White Lotus
An Introduction to Tibetan Culture

White Lotus
An Introduction to Tibetan Culture

Foreword by His Holiness the Dalai Lama

Edited by Carole Elchert
Designed by Philip Sugden

Snow Lion Publications
Ithaca, New York, USA

Snow Lion Publications
P. O. Box 6483
Ithaca, New York 14851
Copyright © 1990 Carole Elchert/Philip Sugden

First Edition U.S.A. 1990

Printed in U.S.A.

ISBN 0-937938-89-0

Library of Congress Cataloging-in-Publication Data

White lotus : an introduction to Tibetan culture / edited by Carole
  Elchert ; foreword by the Dalai Lama ; designed by Philip Sugden. —
  1st ed. U.S.A.
     p.   cm.
  Includes biographical references.
  ISBN 0-937938-89-0
  1. Tibet (China)—Civilization.   I. Elchert, Carole, 1951-
DS786.W426   1990
951'.5—dc20   90-44578
                                         CIP

Cover Photo: *Yarlung Tsangpo, Central Tibet—Philip Sugden*

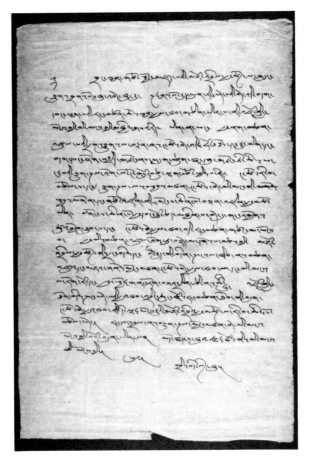

To: The United Nations Organization

This is our most fervent appeal to you. As is well-known throughout the world, Tibet has a long history of independence. However, China, with its brutal military strength, has swallowed our nation and inflicted heart-rending suffering on our people for more than three decades now. In our suffering, we place our hope on His Holiness the Dalai Lama, who—we hope—will deliver us from our long period of sorrow.

We appeal to the United Nations to take an immediate step for the restoration of our independence based on truth, justice and history, and to enable His Holiness the Dalai Lama to return to Tibet. Just as many nations have gained their independence in the light of truth and justice, we hope the United Nations will help in the restoration of Tibet's independence too. This appeal is from all of the people of Tibet—now suffering due to the loss of independence.

With high regards,
People of Markham, Kham, Tibet

Children at Sakya, Tibet

Carole Elchert

This book is dedicated to Tibetans in exile who struggle to keep their culture alive and to those still living in Tibet who struggle to stay alive. It is also dedicated to Robert D. and Martha H. Bright and Elmer and Jean Graham whose belief and generosity helped to make the Cultural Arts Expedition project a reality.

It is our hope that not one voice which cries for freedom and justice goes unheard. We dedicate this book especially to the Khampas of Markham, Tibet, who risked their lives to be heard.

Contents

His Holiness the Dalai Lama   Philip Sugden

THE DALAI LAMA

FOREWORD

The arts have long played a major role in Tibetan culture in the ways we understand and express ourselves and the physical and spiritual aspects of our existence. Similarly, it is through the universal language of art that different peoples and cultures can come to know each other at a deeper, more immediate level.

The 1988 Cultural Arts Expedition had the admirable goal of actively promoting intercultural communication. Such projects are particularly welcome today when distances in space and time are growing ever smaller.

I am, therefore, pleased that *White Lotus*, a video focusing on the Tibetan people and their lives, has been produced by a dedicated team of artists. I believe the video and the book that accompanies it present excellent introductions to our complex culture. Through the images, writings and recordings they contain, viewers and readers will be able to share and participate in something of the experience of being a Tibetan.

July 21, 1990

Preface

On its own, this book is more than an introduction to the land, culture, and people of Tibet. This book is also a photographic and written record of the 1988 Cultural Arts Expedition—a project that materialized from five previous journeys to the Himalayas and took three more years to complete. On the expedition we amassed 20,000 slides of subjects related to Tibetan culture. We covered over 8,000 land miles to photograph in those areas where Tibetan culture still flourishes, including Eastern Tibet and the Central Tibetan plateau (now the Tibetan Autonomous Region under Chinese control), the Himalayan regions where Tibetans migrated over thousands of years, and the exiled communities in India, Nepal, and Ladakh.

Tibet's Buddhist culture evolved from its seventh century C.E. origins when King Songtsen Gampo unified Tibet with a common language and religion. Some Tibetan scholars believe that almost 1,000 years before the reign of Songtsen Gampo, the ancestors of Tibetans were those followers of Rupati who fled the great war with the Pandavas in India (Shakabpa, *Tibet: A Political History*, 1988). For the last two hundred years, mountain ranges and vast upland deserts insulated this Buddhist culture from modernizing forces until the tumultuous invasion of the Communist Chinese in the 1950s. From the '50s on, this ancient culture was thrust into a modern world of machines that promised material progress, resource development that despoiled the environment, and radical changes that translated into cultural disintegration. This book, then, is a tribute to Tibetans' efforts, inside the Chinese-occupied Tibetan Autonomous Region and outside as dispossessed countrymen, to preserve a cultural identity which evolved over three thousand years.

The video, *White Lotus*, presents the culture through images and native sounds; whereas, this companion book provides the balance of information about the Tibetan culture.

PART I contains summaries written by scholars and other authorities. These individual focuses on particular aspects or areas of specialty give the reader a comprehensive view of the Tibetan culture: the history (past and contemporary), customs and lifestyles, ethnic variation, religion, symbols and values, and the arts, including religious arts, architecture, and literature. To avoid overwhelming the reader with complexity and detail, we have pared down the content to the most significant aspects of a culture that arose from its spiritual ideals.

PART II introduces the reader to the story of the 1988 Cultural Arts Expedition, a writer's experiences through journal excerpts, a flutist's inspiration, and the expedition members and authors themselves in biographical paragraphs. Because the video creates an ambience of sight and sound without narration, a description of its content is also included. Finally, we acknowledge the patrons and contributors to this three-year project which, like most projects, begins as inspiration but only achieves realization with the energy, creativity, and support of many individuals. This book is the return on their investment of faith.

Members of the Cultural Arts Expedition with Geshe Ogyen Dorjee, Tinley Sherpa, and Friends at Pangboche Monastery. Photo: Roger Sugden

Introduction
Cultural Arts Expedition Project

Carole Elchert

It was late in the evening before *Losar*, the Tibetan New Year. By the time passing digitally on my watch, it was February 17, 1988. Tibetans follow a shorter, lunar year; their calendar designated the current year as 2115, the Earth Dragon Year. Here in the Information Office of the exiled Tibetan government, a calendar painted in the bold primary colors typical of Tibetan artwork seemed to stand out from a retiring wall. The small print in the bottom corner forecast of 1988: "Extensive disturbances to nature. . .a degenerative era, various diseases like cancer and AIDS will be prevalent . . . the recitation of Vajrapani will be a powerful healing and meditation.''

That same year five artists from three continents met in Delhi, India, to embark on a six-month Cultural Arts Expedition to Tibet and the Himalayas. A year before, the project itself occurred to an artist and a writer from Ohio—Philip Sugden and myself—during a drab spell of rain in February when everyone shares a standard whine about wishing to be elsewhere.

Sipping from a family-size mug that Tibetans offer as a guest's portion of *chang*, their traditional barley drink, I was spending the last night of 2114 inside the Information Office of the Tibetan government-in-exile. While I wrote in my journal, fireworks cracked outside, and streamers of light made the refugee capital—Dharamsala, a former British outpost—visible on the hills of Himachal Pradesh, India. Inside, I doubted my conviction to finish the chang before morning, when four more days of celebrations hosted by the drink would take its toll on reluctant teetotalers. What made temperance improbable was the chang itself. Brewed nearly five months by Pasanng's mother, one in five or six batches was then selected for its sweet though hardly innocent potency. Beyond a precise stage of sweetness, I was told, was a bitter or sour chang that acts as a deathwish whiskey.

Attended by the chang, I sat with an audience of books, magazines, and paper stacks that crowded desks, chairs, and every bit of floor space inside the central government's office. Outside, Tibetans were crowded in mostly two- and three-room homes where a pyramid of stacked crackers and foods, the *dekhae*, were set alongside a canister of barley seedlings on the family's altar. Both were signs of hope and wishes for prosperity. The next day 4,000 Tibetans living in Dharamsala would raise glasses of chang to salute the Earth Dragon Year, expressing what is most painful and yet empowering about life in exile—the waiting. The Tibetan plateau, too, was waiting. Everything piled around that office was waiting for a return to the work of perseverance. For the Tibetans, after almost thirty years in exile from their homeland, ''waiting'' was strewn everywhere in their lives.

In a waiting room mood, I spent that evening worried and restless. After a year of planning and hundreds of letters to organize the project in the U.S. and abroad, I was wondering about our expedition's chance for success. The political situation inside Tibet was volatile at best, and every news day brought a different story about our chances of securing visas from the Chinese government. "No hope," said letters from the U.S., where newscasts compared the Tibet Autonomous Region (TAR) to an inflamed anthill after the October 1987 demonstrations. We'd also heard that the most difficult place to obtain a visa for the TAR was in Kathmandu because the Chinese blamed the "ethnic unrest" on outside agitators. The guilt was conveniently assigned to the younger, independent travelers who congregated in Nepal to gain entry into the still "forbidden kingdom" with its aura of Shangrila. Like them, we planned to get visas in Kathmandu, and we hoped to travel with as few restrictions as possible.

Considering our prospects dim, expedition members were keyed into a tense waiting. Would we be permitted a privileged audience with His Holiness the Dalai Lama? Would we amass enough photographic images and field recordings to produce a thirty-minute video to be broadcast on PBS TV? Would we produce our own work—drawings, writing, music—during a pinballing schedule that took us from India's Karnataka State and the southern refugee communities to Dharamsala; to the blistering cold of Ladakh in winter and back to Delhi's heat; to Nepal and the monasteries and nunneries of the Solu Khumbu; to the plateau of Tibet; and back to the Delhi furnace for a final excursion into Ladakh for the Hemis festival? And would we be able to endure the cramped quarters of each other's company for six months, or would a loss of tolerance literally dismember the expedition? Waiting seemed to be in the cards, and worrying about things ahead wouldn't have made the shuffle turn up anything different.

The next morning produced an auspicious sign for the Cultural Arts Expedition. We were guests of the Tibetan government at a New Year's *puja* (prayer) service conducted by His Holiness on the rooftop of Theckchen Choeling, the main temple in Dharamsala. Only a few guests—mostly the journalist variety—and the administrative arm of the exiled government were permitted to sit with the monks who were chanting prayers to Palden Lhamo, the patron deity of the Tibetan nation.

Not only were we guests for all the New Year's festivities—the dances at a sunrise *sangsol* or incense puja; the New Year's blessing given by the Dalai Lama in his residence to nearly 10,000 people who stood long hours in queues; the fire pujas; the early morning *Ginsek* ceremony; the ritualized bonfires—but we were also the house guests of four couples who were the first generation to graduate from the Tibetans' first school in India at Mussoorie.

We were also invited to photograph the Dalai Lama's private art collection and to photograph and record a full dress rehearsal at the Institute of Performing Arts. At such monasteries as Nechung, we were given the opportunity to photograph and record special services without a second's prior notice. In a festive mood, Tibetans invited us into already overcrowded homes. In Migmar and Wangmo's two rooms, three generations lived and practiced one of the central themes of Mahayana Buddhism—compassion under duress.

Then five days later, Aulde Lelarge (a flutist from Paris) and John Westmore (an Australian painter) stood in traditional gown and chuba (sashed robe) alongside Phil and me for a group photo with the Dalai Lama himself. Our fifteen-minute interview continued for an hour. The video's title—*White Lotus*—was accepted humbly by the "god king" of a people who were, as the lotus symbolizes, rising above historical circumstances and adversity by the flowering of Mahayana Buddhist beliefs in their lives. The leader of the Tibetan nation graciously insisted on pinning an expedition patch to his gown. This gesture of graciousness was repeated by every Tibetan—official or not, titled or untitled—who helped us accomplish our artistic mission over the next five months.

It seemed as though we carried a badge with the face of His Holiness on our requests, our itinerary, our needs; and the Tibetans in India, Ladakh, and Nepal bowed low and performed whatever miracle of diplomacy or maneuvering against a petulant bureaucracy was required.

At Majna ka Tilla, one of the poorest settlements on the outskirts of Delhi, we photographed faces smiling despite the abject conditions.

In the Hunsur settlements of Rabgayling and Bylakuppe in Southern India, carpet weavers sang traditional songs to oblige my recording urge, which, by then, had become an addiction. Six-year-old Tenzin Gakyi, whose name means happiness, sang at full-lung capacity the popular tune calling for Tibet's independence. (Three months later in the back streets of Lhasa, we heard the same tune hummed under pilgrims' breath.) I hesitated to ask for a simple recording session at Sera, now the largest extant Mahayana Buddhist monastery and a sister to the one outside Lhasa. Sera's three abbots who were escorting us on a tour of the grounds, however, immediately summoned some of the 1,000 resident Gelukpa (Yellow Hat) monks from their nightly bouts of ritual debate. In less than five minutes, 600 monks were seated in the main chapel and waiting for my diffident finger to orchestrate an on-the-spot recording of a special occasion chant, the "Short Steps to Liberation."

That evening when the electricity went off, the abbots guided us by flashlight into a small chapel. Under a blinding spotlight that made grotesque forms of the shadows, each abbot spoke about the abuses of human rights in Tibet, the genocide, the imprisonments, the suffocation of a culture through laws and intimidation. They told their personal stories and described the destruction of monasteries in Tibet. One of the abbots watched us, smiling as though he understood that we were no longer in the dark about Tibet.

Everywhere in the southern settlements, expedition members were received like dignitaries, not only by His Holiness's representatives but by the abbots of monasteries who offered the obligatory tea. In fact, one teacup seemed to spill over into another monastery and another session with the rinpoche or abbot. In the Kagyudpa Monastery, the Venerable K.C. Ayang spoke with us in the hypnotic tones of a voice long conditioned by prayer and puja services. His specialty is the *Phowa* teaching which prepares a person for right action at death, reminding us that there is an art to living and to leaving, to the performance and to the stage exit.

For six uninterrupted days in the southern settlements, Phil Sugden photographed artwork, portraits, puja services, rug weavers and other handicrafts, while I followed with two professional Sony recorders on cue at all times. At the Sakya Monastery, a pair of traditional felt boots—the colorful stripes in sharp contrast to a dull grey floorboard—caught our photographic attention. What we considered photo-worthy for aesthetic reasons was often questioned by Tibetan bystanders. The good-humored Tibetans laughed uncontrollably the moment Phil began to take shots of those boots, which are as ordinary to Tibetans as drying dung on a southerly wall.

On the way back to Bangalore, our Khampa driver faced traffic and swerved from oncoming traffic with undaunted confidence. Like every other driver on Indian roadways, he played a kind of open road "chicken" that is not only necessary for survival, but allows people the exhilaration of living just one second before the final impact with death.

On that ride, we witnessed a sign fraught with meaning (or of the innate humor of the cosmos) in an otherwise haphazard sequence of events. The banana peel that I handed Phil to toss out his window was charmed by the alignment of grubby paws. Phil tossed the peel in the direction of a rhesus monkey perched atop a garbage heap. Not counting on its luck, the monkey was sitting on its haunches and facing the sun with arms outstretched in the standard gesture of supplication. Amazingly, the banana peel arched through the air and landed in its hands. The monkey jumped back, even more astonished than we were by the immediate reply to his pleas. The next time he petitions the gods, though, he'll probably order a more substantial meal. Although the incident seemed clearly marked as a sign, members were unsure if the sign was meant for the expedition or for the hopeful monkey.

After visiting the Tibetan settlements of South India, we spent several weeks in Dharamsala. Aulde and John stayed there to produce artwork and study at the Institute of Performing Arts. Phil and I caught one of the few flights that actually landed at the Leh airport; many scheduled flights return without landing because of the severe weather in February. The winter world of Ladakh is a landscape barren of tourists and scant of heat; a small woodstove's output is limited by the unavailability of fuel on this high altitude desert. Temperatures at night drop well below minus ten degrees Fahrenheit. The cold refutes the manufacturers' claims that two layers of comforters, a down sleeping bag, and thermal underwear will keep us warm. The days, however, are cloudless and 25 ASA bright, ideal conditions for winter photography of the highest inhabited place on earth.

We lived in the S.O.S. Children's Village, one of approximately ten Tibetan settlements dispersed over the Indus River Valley near Leh. With a Tibetan guide, we photographed ancient monasteries, including Spitok, Thikse, Stakna, and Hemis. In Leh, we photographed the Shey palace overlooking that flat-roofed town, the Jokhang Temple in the heart of Leh, and dozens of relocated Tibetans, many of whom were nomads from Western Tibet.

One evening, I recorded the traditional songs and instrumentation of a master teacher, Dorjee Gyaltsen. After crouching for a day in the open-air bed of a truck, he'd just returned to Choglamsar from winter holidays with his family, who were nomads on the remote Chang Tang plateau. Living on those bitter cold upland plains, I thought, seemed to prepare Tibetans for a ride even a hitchhiking yak with an opposable thumb would refuse. We sat long hours with Tibetans like Tenzin, the principal at S.O.S. school, and listened to wisdom such as this disguised as humor: "It's sometimes the pleasure of others to make you miserable; it's your responsibility to make yourself happy." And we heard tales of exiled Tibetans who disguised themselves as nomads and crossed the Indian borders illegally to visit relatives and sacred places in Tibet. Every minute of their journey was raw with the possibility of discovery and then imprisonment or execution.

The highlight of our winter stay in Ladakh was the annual oracle and festival at Matho Monastery. To avoid the displeasure of two sword-bearing monks, their bodies energized by powerful tantric deities (*lhas*) which enter them during a two-day trance, we photographed from inside a stall once used as a toilet. Monks assured us that, although the lhas were sometimes enraged by cameras and other invading technologies, they would not defile themselves by attacking us there. The day before, however, a Sony recorder was spotted by one of the frenzied oracles, and a 300 year-old sword slashed across its casing, but only put the record function out of commission. With accuracy like that, we decided, it made no sense to annoy the swordbearer.

Then back to Delhi and, with photographer Roger Sugden, the expedition moved on to Kathmandu and the Solu Khumbu region of Nepal. One afternoon, at the Boudhinath Tibetan settlement, a sudden violent hailstorm ended in a full rainbow from the largest Buddhist stupa (shrine) in the world to a nearby gompa (monastery). The three people photographing the scene were Roger Sugden, myself, and Mani Lama. Mani Lama, the Tibetan whose images appear on most of the postcards sold in Nepal, told me that this was a rare and fortunate event in his lifetime of photographing Tibetan subject matter.

In the Everest region of Nepal, where high mountain valleys are inhabited by the Sherpa who came from Eastern Tibet over 300 years ago, we were escorted by a young monk named Tinley from Tyangboche Monastery. With the blessings of Tyangboche's incarnate lama, Nawang Tenzin, we photographed and recorded at 100-, 200-, and 300-year-old *gompas* (monasteries), including Thame, Pang-boche, and the Debuche nunnery. Many of the older nuns who fled from Rong-buck Monastery at the base of Mt. Everest, one of the 6,000 monasteries in Tibet razed during the Cultural Revolution, now live in Debuche. Inside a small stone hut, a nun lived in self-imposed confinement so that she could meditate un-disturbed for the rest of her life. I was struck with the thought that the woman could only see the stunning moss-draped forest and the Himalayan peaks through the bars of her monastic vow.

At Pangboche, Roger photographed ancient dance masks of carved wood. Then we met with Geshe Ogyen Dorjee, who lived in that 13,000-foot Himalayan vil-lage at the same altitude as his homeland, the Tibetan plateau. To acquire the scholarship rank of *geshe* he had studied extensively in three Buddhist schools—the Nyingmapa, Sakyapa and Katumpu, the older Gelugpa school—before flee-ing Tibet twenty-nine years earlier. For many years in Nepal, his geshe status was undisclosed while he struggled to survive as a field laborer. With a passion for debate, the geshe challenged us about photographing Tibetan portraits when—in his opinion—every human face was individual. He asserted that there simply wasn't a prototypic Tibetan face. Phil conceded the point and ended the discus-sion by clapping his hands in the ritual fashion of Gelugpa debaters. The geshe was delighted with his easy victory over the camera crew but then insisted we take his photograph.

Those four weeks in Himalayan villages allowed us to produce work for an April 15 opening at the American Culture Center in Kathmandu. The exhibition represented the five artists' work in Nepal: Phil Sugden's sepia ink drawings, John Westmore's pastels and watercolors, Roger Sugden's black and white pho-tography, Aulde LeLarge's flute compositions, and my prose pieces. The speak-er that evening, the Chancellor of the Art Academy, called for more artistic conquests of his country, more cultural arts expeditions like our own.

It was the fourth month of the expedition, and after waiting three weeks in Kathmandu for the Chinese to open Tibet's borders, we were tired and yet anx-ious to move on. For several months, tourists were being denied access to Tibet, as journalists had been for over a year. Demonstrations during the Tibetans' March Monlam festival had not given tourist the ''correct'' impression, so the Chinese wanted some time to apply a veneer over the widespread discontent of Tibetans.

Meanwhile, we investigated the usual and some desperate ways to secure a visa: a single, Chinese-approved tour package deal, which we couldn't afford (over $100/day); the promise of the Chinese road-building crew to help us obtain a special permit from Lhasa (which Nepalese tour agents assured us was a hoax since Lhasa telex and phone lines were not being answered); and the backstreet agencies who deal in hopeless schemes. After a strange set of circumstances and an opportune, chance meeting with a Frenchman late one evening, we discovered that he indeed was able to get visas and guarantee our entry into Tibet. What he promised was that we would be traveling as a small group, at budget rates artists could not resist, and just one day after the borders officially opened—everything that we had been told was impossible. At that time the official Chinese response to events in Tibet was capricious, and so one week after we entered Tibet the borders were again closed to travelers because of a swell of protests.

Finally one day in May, we watched as a monstrously long CAC 707 landed on a perilously short Kathmandu runway. The expedition members doubted this strange luck that would permit the four of us and one Nepalese businessman to board the plane for Lhasa. Such trickling tourism as this was a problem most likely caused by a flood tide of Chinese greed: A plane that should have been packed twice weekly was nearly empty because the Chinese courted big-dollar tour groups. Those groups were reluctant, though, to enter the troubled land, and budget travelers, who were insincere capitalists by Chinese standards but itching to cross the border, were denied access.

Once in Lhasa, our problems only started. We first convinced skeptical customs officials that 400 rolls of film were to be divided up between four ordinary, eager-to-photograph tourists. The Chinese are always on guard for any group or individual who might profit from a photographic vantage of Tibet's "medieval" society. To the Chinese, Tibet is an open-air museum, which they open and close to visiting audiences at their discretion and convenience.

A week later at the Lhasa tour agency, we conducted a minor protest about having a Chinese driver. Since one Chinese in 1,400 has a driver's license, the person with a license in China is viewed as a minor deity and acts the part. On the first scheduled trip to the Lake Namtso nomad camps, our Chinese driver passed whatever we wanted to photograph; drove recklessly over nomads' pasturelands, once hitting a dog that could have easily been seen on an upland plain stretching for fifty miles in every direction. Our Tibetan interpreter flared red but remained quiet when the Chinese driver laughed aloud. The next day, though, our protest resulted in our having a Tibetan driver for the remainder of the trip. Good natured and obliging, Dawa even apologized when he braked once for a photostop, and the only telephone pole in ten miles stood outside my window, obstructing my view.

On a limiting thirty-day schedule, I was able to photograph most of the major monasteries and temples of Central Tibet, including Tsurphu, Drigung, Tidrom nunnery, Ganden, Sera, Drepung, Potala, Palalubu, Jokhang, Nechung, Samye, Sakya, Samding, Shalu, the Kumbum in Gyantse, and Tashilhunpo in Shigatse. Our itinerary allowed us to sketch and photograph at historical sites, like Yumbulagang in the Yarlung Valley. We were exhausted by hours and days of travel on bone-jarring gravel roads to such isolated areas as the Lake Namtso nomad camps and Rongbuck Monastery at the northern base of Mt. Everest.

In Tibet, two incidents, among the blatantly obvious ones, attested to the Tibetans' rejection of their questionable "autonomous status" under Beijing's complete control. On May 17, we had an unscheduled day in Lhasa because Phil had to make a return trip to Drigung Monastery to find a lost money pouch and our travel permits. This meant travelling an additional eight hours on top of the four-hour return trip to Lhasa the morning of the 16th. Every one of the monks at Drigung turned up to look for the missing pouch. With contents intact, the pouch was discovered under the thick quilts we had used the night before.

On our last day in Lhasa the next morning, I intended to make a final round with circumambulating pilgrims on the Barkhor. This street rings the sacred Jokhang Cathedral. Suddenly, shop doors were flung shut, crowds stepped back, and thirteen nuns with hands and voices raised in peaceful protest began to circle the Barkhor. A woman grabbed me and gasping, said that "police come now." I followed the nuns, hoping that plain clothes police who could be standing among the aloof and frightened bystanders would not spot me. On the nuns' third round of the Barkhor—where worshippers and protestors walked side-by-side—Chinese police fired a volley of warning shots above the plaza crowds, circled the nuns, and arrested them. I'll never forget the cries of Tibetan women as they huddled against the doors of the Jokhang temple, which was locked to protect its contents. Nor can I forget the frightened faces of young Chinese soldiers as they fired above the waves of screaming, retreating crowds.

The most incongruous sight was the group of tourists who strolled through the gunfire and the smoke screen of bombs. The tourists passed a Tibetan woman who stood vulnerable on the pile of rocks being used to rebuild the Jokhang and never glanced in her direction. This solitary woman, perhaps representing seven million Tibetans in a world of billions, stood witness to her kinsmen's sacrifices for independence. She watched over events often ignored by nations that stand by as casual and detached as those tourists were from the crisis in Tibet.

Several days before, a note that turned out to be an appeal for human rights from the people of Kham, Eastern Tibet, was stuffed inside Phil's pocket while he sketched one of Tibet's most sacred sites. (The letter, addressed to the Secretary General of the United Nations, appears in the Foreword of this book.) We were told that persons delivering such notes were risking their lives for a chance to be heard by the world community. Thus tourists inside Tibet were assuming the journalists' role of witnessing and reporting.

After Tibet, three expedition members—Phil Sugden, John Westmore, and I—went to Ladakh. There Phil photographed the ancient, rarely published murals of Alchi, and I photographed and recorded the mask dances at the Hemis festival. The miraculous occurred, as it often did on this expedition, one evening while I was passing time with the ordinary. One black and another white horse met in front of my camera's lens and touched necks just as the evening light cast Lamayuru Monastery in gold. A Cibachrome print of this fortunate conjunction is entitled "East Meets West."

We mistakenly concluded that no landscape could match the spectacular sunrises and sunsets at the oldest holy site in Ladakh, Lamayuru Monastery, which rests in a cradle of snowpeaks. Then we took the jeep ride on the road from Leh to Srinigar. After twenty-four hours and the hairpin curves of the highest road on earth, open only three months of the year, my earlier verdict and stomach were both overturned.

By the expedition's end in Ladakh, Philip Sugden had completed 135 sepia ink drawings, and John Westmore had finished 140 ink, pastel, and charcoal studies—preliminaries for works they would later complete at studios in Findlay and Melbourne. Aulde Lelarge had composed nearly twenty pieces for flute based on her experiences and traditional Tibetan music. Between photographing and recording over 1500 minutes of sounds, I was able to complete two mostly thick and sometimes inspired journals. The expedition was to go home with 17,000 slide images—the combined effort of Phil in India, Roger in Nepal, and me in Tibet.

So after the waiting in airports, the waiting to gain entry into Tibet, the waiting in queued-up India, we'd completed the 1988 Cultural Arts Expedition by July 14, 1988.

Once home, we renewed our funding efforts, and waiting was again the accompaniment to all our actions. In April 1989, the Ohio Arts and Humanities Councils' Joint Program, the National Endowment of the Humanities, WBGU TV studios in Bowling Green, Ohio, awarded the Cultural Arts Project funds to produce the video for broadcast. We spent another year in Bowling Green's WBGU TV studio to complete the video by the autumn of 1990 for the Inaugural Opening at The University of Findlay.

Then in May 1989, I joined a three-week Power Places tour of Eastern Tibet—the regions of Amdo and Kham which were annexed to mainland China. The itinerary included the bamboo forests of Jiuzhaigou (the ''Nine Tibetan Village'' nature preserve), Amdo's Labrang and Kumbum monasteries, and the remote highland pastures around Rorgai, where nomad clans moving their herds of yaks to summer pasture encountered westerners (our group) for the first time. After passing through some of the major cities of China, where student and worker demonstrations joined the clamor for democracy in the streets of Lhasa, I returned with 1,000 additional images for the Cultural Arts slide library and multi-media and book projects.

Like the Tibetans in exile and those enduring the calamitous presence of the Chinese Communists on the Tibetan plateau, the members of an artistic expedition had, by the journey's end, become inured to waiting. What we'd learned from the Tibetans, though, was that waiting is the greater and more instructive part of work. What I saw on a billboard in India but more clearly saw in the actions of Tibetans who helped us on this project was that "work is worship." Looking back over three years of work, I discovered that in the time it takes for a project to complete its course, a people to regain their sovereignty and their homeland, or a newborn yak to grow into a harness is either a lifetime of duty performed without pleasure or a single second of rarefied delight.

PART I

1 *Tibetan History*

Lobsang Lhalungpa

Tibet is a vast country in Central Asia with a history of over three thousand years. Its location, on the high plateau, surrounded by mountain ranges, has kept Tibet generally isolated from the rest of the world and has allowed a homogeneous society to create and nurture a rich, spiritual tradition.

Tibet's southern border is formed by the outer ranges of the Himalaya; the western border by the Karakoram range; the northern frontier by the Altyn Tagh range (which borders on Chinese Turkestan); and the Eastern border along what old Tibetan documents call "an iron bridge and a white stupa" in Tachinlu (near the Chinese provinces of Szechuan and Singkiang).

Four of India's great rivers originate in the vicinity of Mt. Kailash, a sacred mountain to both Hindus and Buddhists, in the Western Tibetan highlands: the Indus, the Sutlej, the Ganges and the Brahmaputra. Burma's Salween River springs from Central Tibet. The two Tibetan rivers, Ngochu and Dzachu, merge in Eastern Tibet to form the Mekong River of Laos and Thailand. China's mighty Yangtse traces its source to the Drichu, which originates in the Northern Tibetan highlands, while the Yellow River (Huang-ho) starts as the Machu River in the vicinity of sacred Mt. Amnye in Tibet's northeastern region of Amdo.

Tibetans call their country "the Land of Snowy Mountains and Healing Plants." Contrary to popular misconceptions, Tibet is blessed with natural splendor and rich resources. Its geographical features comprise three general areas:

The high Northern plateau is a land of shimmering glaciers, vast sandy steppes and turquoise lakes. It is known for its harsh climate during the long winter months when fierce blizzards howl across the Northern highlands.

In the subtropical conditions of the South and East, one finds a beautiful landscape of snow-capped mountains, waterfalls, pine, juniper or aspen forests, green valleys, streams and lakes. This area includes Tibet's rich, fertile farmlands. Eastern Tibet is also home to the martial and enterprising Khampas.

The third climatic zone, the U and Tsang regions of Central Tibet has at its heart the holy city of Lhasa (built during the seventh century C.E.). Very different geographical conditions prevail here. An amphitheater of mountains encloses green valleys, lakes and rivers. The sun-drenched, south-facing mountainsides are mostly barren, whereas the shady sides are lined with alpine meadows where medicinal plants grow in profusion. The valleys in this region are fertile on account of the many rivers crossing them. The inhabitants of Central Tibet are considered gentle and religious.

All Tibet was once a land of pristine purity due to sparse population and the people's inbred sense of respect for nature and an ecological balance. The origins of this reverence can be found in Tibet's early beliefs, the native Bon religion. This pre-Buddhist nature worship propounded the concept of cosmic cohabitation. The physical world was considered not only the heavenly abode of the cosmic deities but also the sacred habitat of all living beings. All mountains, lakes, rivers, trees, and even the elements were sacred dwellings of the spiritual forces; indeed, the entire country was deemed a "sacred realm." Especially hallowed were the great mountains, such as Amnye Machen in the East, Jomo Langmo (Mt. Everest) in the West, Nyachen Thanglha to the North, and Jomo Lhari to the South.

Much like American Indians, Tibetans consciously lived a simple life and avoided any senseless exploitation of their natural resources. They pursued a spiritual life, in harmony with the surrounding elements, instead of competing with the outside world in industry and commerce.

Yumbulagang Monastery, Yarlung, Tibet.　　　　　　　Photo: Carole Elchert

Yet this pre-Buddhist culture, even though simple, was not primitive in the sense of a stone-age society. During this early part of their history, Tibetans made and used articles for utilitarian purposes and worship or decoration. A variety of ritual objects, musical instruments, dance costumes, and masks were made out of woven cloth, wood, or metal. Weapons, such as swords, lances and armor, were crafted for warriors and their horses. Beautifully decorated handicrafts were an integral part of the lives of nomads and villagers. Woolen clothes, blankets, leather implements and tools of all kinds were produced. In addition to water-proof tents made out of yak hair by the nomads, the early Tibetans constructed brick houses. Numerous watchtowers and fortresses guarded important caravan routes and settlements. (The ruins of many of these survived up to recent times.) Communities were led by elders, chiefs, and priests with warriors, healers, diviners, and oracles playing an active role. In addition, musicians, storytellers, dancers, and craftsmen were highly regarded.

The basic philosophy of this early cultural tradition propounded ways by which humans, as heavenly subjects, could best maintain a harmonious relationship with their protective deities on the one hand and with their natural environment on the other. Great emphasis was placed on loyalty to family, community, and monarch. The phenomena of the external world also represented a kind of cosmic temple. Reverence for and preservation of natural resources was a religious obligation, as humans were considered the conscientious custodians of nature's treasures. In addition, the Bon culture placed great emphasis on ethics, especially honesty and honor. The fulfillment of personal honor, however, often caused people to resort to violence as warriors valiantly defended their personal or family honor. If such an act was truly justifiable, it had religious sanction and social approval.

The ancient culture was concerned with practical ways of meeting individuals' and society's needs for well-being, security, justice, and harmony. Education was based on the rich oral tradition and social interaction. Religious studies centered on the Bon faith, its philosophy, cosmogony, pantheon, rituals, liturgy, music, dance, and the arts of divining and healing. Secular education consisted of the ancient wisdom, folklore, songs, epics, crafts, eloquence in story-telling, and poetry. This knowledge was transmitted by married priests to their children and devotees. The ancient tradition emphasized eighteen aspects: nine belonged to the martial arts system (specifying the mastery of physical prowess, weight lifting, running, archery, and swordsmanship) and nine were concerned with oratory, sagacity, and chivalry. No distinctions were made in education between men and women. Women in ancient Tibetan society enjoyed far more equality than in the so-called advanced civilizations. In addition to shouldering domestic chores, women participated in economic, social, and religious activities on an equal basis with men and were treated with respect.

The most important phase of Tibet's history began during the seventh century C.E. under the great King Songtsen Gampo (thirty-seven in line of the ancient Miyilha Dynasty). Originally his authority was confined to South Tibet, but during his military campaigns into neighboring territories, he came in contact with the great civilizations of India, China, Nepal, and Central Asia. He was particularly impressed with the Buddhist tradition and culture. As a man of vision, Songtsen

Potala Palace, Lhasa.   Ink Drawing—Philip Sugden

Gampo then set four major goals for himself: successful unification of the numerous principalities and tribes throughout Tibet into one strong, dynamic nation; the growth of the new nation into a formidable military power and expansion into neighboring states; the establishment of a politico-religious tradition; and the religious and cultural transformation of his subjects. Having accomplished these goals and successfully unifying Tibet, the king led the Tibetan army in the conquest of neighboring countries. For a considerable time during the seventh and eighth centuries, Tibet controlled extensive areas of both China and India, parts of Burma, and all of Nepal. Next, he established the institution described as the twin system of temporal and spiritual authority with the monarch himself embodying this authority. (This system has been followed by all subsequent rulers up to the present time.)

He then initiated a major movement to bring Buddhism to Tibet. As the most important step towards this goal, the king decided to have a Tibetan national script invented so that the Tibetan language with its rich and refined oral tradition could be a vehicle for teaching and translating. For this purpose, he sent two groups of bright young men to Buddhist centers in India to study Sanskrit and Buddhism. Only a few, however, survived the heat of the plains and were able to return as accomplished teachers and translators. One such translator was Thonmi (who later became the able minister for religion and culture). He invented the thirty-four letter alphabet which he modeled loosely after an Indian Gupta script. He also composed the first Tibetan grammar. The king then commissioned a translation program led by an international Buddhist team which collaborated with Tibetan translators. A number of Buddhist treatises (sutras) were successfully translated into Tibetan and many manuscripts were produced. The king and his Newari queen themselves are said to have studied Buddhism and the new script together. Classical Tibetan thus became the effective medium of communication and intellectual expansion and has remained one of the unifying factors throughout Tibet's history.

In the meantime, the king focused his attention on the construction of Buddhist temples throughout his realm. The "Central Temple" (Tibetan: Jokhang) and the Ramoche Temple became shrines for two large Buddha statues brought by the King's two Buddhist queens from their homelands: Nepal and China. The statues were believed to have been sculpted during the time of the historical Buddha and blessed by Him. They were given to Chinese and Newari rulers by a king of Magadha (the modern state of Bihar). The king even had the foresight to have treasures of precious gems concealed in the Central Temple for future renovation purposes. These two temples, together with the Potala Palace which was also built around that time, have always been revered by Tibetans and fellow Buddhists as sacred places. Songtsen Gampo then had the city of Lhasa built around these holy temples in the Kyisho Valley. (Lhasa was to remain the capital for the next three centuries and would again become the capital from the seventeenth century to the present.)

As Buddhist temples sprang up all over the country, ordinary Tibetans became acquainted with the emerging Buddhist tradition. Songtsen Gampo proclaimed the ten noble Buddhist principles and the sixteen humanistic deeds, all based on the principles of non-violence and compassion, to be the official code of ethics.

Hum The Immovable.   Oil—John Westmore

He also established a new educational system suited to Tibetan ingenuity and needs. Artisans from Nepal, Central Asia, and India were engaged to train Tibetans. Tibetan students were sent to China to learn the arts of porcelain making and silk weaving, among others. The king had valuable Buddhist manuscripts (mostly in Sanskrit), sacred images, artifacts, and ritual objects brought to Lhasa from India and other neighboring countries. (This practice was to be followed by subsequent rulers.)

During his rule Songtsen Gampo accomplished the goals he had set out for himself mainly because of his vision and determination. His royal patronage and protection made the entire effort progress successfully. Thus, a sound foundation for the newly unified nation was established.

After King Songtsen Gampo's death, several generations of rulers failed to give strong support to the new faith until, finally, Buddhism again found a powerful patron in the person of King Trisong Detsen (755-797). He organized the construction of the first Buddhist monastery, Samye, fifty miles south of Lhasa, and twelve Buddhist centers in other areas. Samye became an important center of international Buddhist activities. Artisans and teachers from India, Central Asia, Nepal, Kashmir, and China were invited to this first great Buddhist monastic university in Tibet. Samye had departments for different branches of learning, translation, meditation, medicine, art, and other studies. Tibetan teachers and translators, such as Bairochana, were assisted by a team of Buddhist teachers from other countries. The great Indian savant, Santaraksita, presided as the chief abbot over the ordination of the first and successive groups of young Tibetans into the monastic order. While they successfully completed their religious training and became learned scholars, other Tibetans followed in their footsteps. Santaraksita propagated the Buddhist teachings, but since they dealt with rationalism and morality (originating from the sutras), they drew negative reactions from the ritual-loving populace, still steeped in the Bon tradition. Santaraksita felt that the success of orthodox Buddhism could only be assured by bringing in Buddhist mysticism, whose apparent ritualistic and formal affinity with the animistic Bon cult would reassure its believers. Hence, he advised King Trisong Detsen to invite Padmasambhava, a great Indian master of Buddhist mysticism, to come to Tibet. This great teacher, renowned for having performed many miracles, came to Tibet and remained there for many years. He was able not only to convince the skeptics but to bring them into the Buddhist fold.

Padmasambhava was the person who introduced an important branch of the Buddhist Supreme Yoga (Tantra) to Tibet. The practice of this new system was said to bring about rapid enlightenment and, since it was not subject to monastic ordination, the Tantra system was made available to lay people. Having achieved enlightenment, the first group of twenty-five initiates then propagated the Buddhist Supreme Yoga. Revered as the original lineage of the first Tibetan Buddhist order, the Nyingmapa (the Upholders of the Ancient Doctrine) were a mixed group of men and women of both royal and common background. Foremost among them were King Trisong Detsen and Lady Yeshe Tsogyal. The latter became Tibet's first woman teacher and recorded in writing the secret oral teachings of Padmasambhava for posterity (in coded language). These teachings were buried, along with sacred images, in many different locations throughout Tibet, to be found centuries later by various reincarnations of Padmasambhava.

Translations of the major Buddhist texts from Sanskrit and Chinese were continued by a team of Tibetan translators under the guidance of their Buddhist teachers. Subsequent Tibetan teachers and modern Western scholars have acclaimed these translations as being excellent and inspiring in terms of their accuracy and quality.

Several generations after King Trisong Detsen, the Buddhist movement received a new impetus under King Tri Ralpachen (805-838). He, too, patronized many important Buddhist activities. One notable program was the reform of the Tibetan language and the standardization of the technical terms which contributed to the advancement of translation, both in terms of quality and quantity. With the assassination of the king by supporters of his disgruntled elder brother, Lang Darma, the latter became ruler in 842. As part of his revenge, Lang Darma engaged in vicious persecution of Buddhists. But before long, the apostate ruler himself fell at the hands of a Buddhist monk. One of Lang Darma's sons, Prince Osung, then set up what came to be called the Guge Kingdom in Western Tibet. His descendants eventually played a vital role in the revival of Buddhism.

The success of this Buddhist renaissance was mainly due to the various Tibetan Buddhist orders and the many teachers and translators. During this period many new orders emerged, of which four major ones still exist today: the Nyingmapa (The Ancient Ones); the Kagyupa (The Order of Secret Oral Transmission); the Sakyapa (The White Earth Order); and the Gelukpa (The Virtuous Order). Also still existing alongside them is the pre-Buddhist Bon Order.

This historical development led to the transformation of the Tibetan people into a more peaceful nation, and their culture into a more refined way of life. The harmonious blending of the Buddhist tradition with the native Bon culture and elements of different neighboring civilizations led to a unique society.

From the tenth century, Buddhism continued to spread not only throughout Tibet but also through neighboring states, especially Mongolia and China. In time, there were more than 6,000 monasteries in Tibet, many of them major religious centers. Monasteries and the homes of wealthy individuals became repositories of libraries, sacred artifacts, and religious treasures.

After the decline of Tibet's Miyilha Dynasty, Tibet once again returned to a system of self-governing states and principalities. This situation came to an end in 1254, when Chogyal Phagpa, a high Lama of the Sakyapa Order of Tibetan Buddhism, was installed as the sovereign ruler of Tibet by the Mongol Kublai Khan, a grandson of Genghis Khan. Successive lamas of the Sakyapa Order were to rule Tibet for the next 96 years from their stronghold in the Sakya area of Tsang (Western Tibet). But despite the fact that, during the next 400 years, political fortunes changed several more times in Tibet, resulting in setbacks or oblivion for the defeated rulers, Buddhism continued to spread due to the support and faith of the people.

Beginning in 1358, the Sakyapa Order lost its political power to Pagdru Jangchub Gyaltsen, a sagacious prince and the head of the Phagdru branch of the Kagyupa Order, whose power base was at Nedong, in the U region of Central Tibet. Phagdru Jangchub Gyaltsen was later hailed by Tibetans as having been the most able and enlightened ruler Tibet had seen since the ancient kings. Phagdru's descendants ruled Tibet for 149 years, although their prestige and power gradually declined. By 1498, one of their officials administered the Rinpung District of Tsang (he adopted the name Rinpung) and usurped power, reducing the Phagdru rulers to a ceremonial role. Beginning in 1566, Tsetan Dorje of Tsang, a subordinate of Rinpung, gradually seized control of more areas until he became the ruler of Tsang. For about a century under the latter two lay rulers, Central Tibet (i.e., the regions of U and Tsang) experienced much instability owing to interregional feuds. Rinpung and Tsetan Dorje's harassment of the Gelukpa monasteries around Lhasa (in U) and Tashilhunpo (in Tsang) aggravated the already volatile situation. Both of those ruling families were zealous supporters of an older and more ambitious Karma Kagyupa Order.

As the oppression of the Gelukpa monks intensified and threatened their very survival, the Gelukpas solicited the support of a number of Mongol Khans who were staunch Gelukpa supporters. Finally, in 1642, the Tsang ruler and his supporters were overthrown by a combined army of Mongol tribes and by Tibetan troops from the U region of Tibet. The fifth Dalai Lama was proclaimed the temporal and spiritual ruler of Tibet.

The title Dalai Lama (literally, "Ocean of Wisdom") had been conferred upon

Samye Monastery, Tibet.   Photo: Carole Elchert

the third Grand Lama, Sonam Gyatso, by Altan Khan of the Tumat Mongol tribe in 1578 in recognition of the Lama's successful conversion of the Mongolians to the Gelukpa faith. The title was then posthumously applied to previous incarnations.

Some Dalai Lamas died young. During the next centuries, whenever there was no Dalai Lama or he was still too young to rule, the National Assembly would appoint a high lama as regent. Unfortunately, some of these regents turned out to be bad rulers, due to their incompetency or to corruption. The present four-teenth Dalai Lama, who has been living in exile in India since 1959, comes from an ordinary peasant family in Eastern Tibet and is highly revered by Tibetans everywhere.

The successive governments under the Dalai Lamas have brought stability and prosperity to Tibet. Even though the socio-political system was not democratic, neither was it "feudal" in the traditional sense of the term. More than 50 percent of Tibet's high-level officials and almost 100 percent of the middle and lower level officials were selected from among ordinary people. Literacy and social mobility were higher than in many developing countries. There was never any shortage of food until after the Chinese invasion in the 1950s.

The political status of Tibet has continuously been misunderstood, mainly because of its isolationist policy before the turn of the century. Tibet was an independent state, with a small national army, its own communications system, and its own foreign relations policies. Since the eighteenth century, various Chinese rulers had deliberately created the impression that Tibet was—and always had been—a part of China. Contacts between China and Tibet go back to the very early period between 1028 and 257 B.C.E. when, according to ancient Chinese records, the Tibetan Ch'iang and other tribes traded in Szechuan, Kansu, Shansi, and Shensi. The Tibetan warrior chief, Fu Chien, even created his own empire in northern China for a short time. Later, Sino-Tibetan relations can be roughly divided into the four following phases, each of which reflected the strength or weaknesses of one side or the other.

During the first phase, between the seventh and ninth centuries, relations were based on the principle of equality. The mighty D'ang Emperors were compelled to accept this by virtue of Tibet's great military power.

The second phase took place during the thirteenth century when China lost its independence to the Mongol conquerors. Tibet had earlier accepted the supremacy of Genghis Khan. Kublai Khan, grandson of Genghis Khan, became emperor of China's Yuan Dynasty. He appointed a high lama of the Sakya Order, Chogyal Phagpa, as imperial preceptor and regent of Tibet. The special relationship between these two leaders was based on an ancient Buddhist tradition known as the "patron-saint relationship." The emperor accepted the lama as his saintly teacher, pledging moral and material support to him and to Tibetan Buddhism. But once the Mongol ruler was overthrown, Tibet also became free of the Mongol overlordship.

The third phase of Sino-Tibetan relations was once again based on the mutual acceptance of the status of equality. The move was initiated by the Manchu emperor, Shun Chih (1653), who lavished on the fifth Dalai Lama honor and hospitality worthy of a foreign sovereign. The emperor and the Dalai Lama met as two sovereigns on thrones of equal height. The Dalai Lama obliged the emperor with Buddhist blessings and teachings, as he had been proclaimed the imperial preceptor. For China, this was part of a grand strategy for pacifying the ever troublesome Mongol warriors, since the Dalai Lama had tremendous influence in Mongolia.

During the fourth phase of Sino-Tibetan relations, this special relationship deteriorated after the death of the fifth Dalai Lama. The Chinese indulged in intrigues by playing the Tibetan ruling elite against the descendants of Gosri Khan, who had been instrumental in installing the fifth Dalai Lama as sovereign ruler of Tibet. Chinese troops invaded Tibet a number of times under the pretext of maintaining peace and protecting the sacred person of the Dalai Lama, while the representative of the Manchu emperor sought in vain to interfere in Tibetan affairs. Tibet finally expelled the Chinese troops in 1913, when the last Manchu emperor was overthrown. That year, the thirteenth Dalai Lama re-established Tibet's independence. However, in 1950-51, soon after mainland China fell into the hands of the Chinese Communists, the Red Army invaded and occupied Tibet.

Tibet fared better in its relations with a number of other neighboring countries. Tibet had a special treaty of mutual support with Mongolia before the Communists overran that country and a similar treaty with Nepal. After the British invasion of Tibet in 1904, which was designed to eliminate what was perceived as a Russian foothold in Tibet, Tibet and Britain signed two treaties. The British, like other Western governments, had been misled by the Chinese. They discovered not only that there was no Russian foothold in Tibet, but also that Tibet was managing its affairs as a sovereign and independent state. Tibet, however, did maintain periodic diplomatic contact with Czar Nicholas II.

By 1950-51 the Communist Red Army had invaded and occupied Tibet. In 1959 the Communist suppressed a popular uprising in Lhasa, causing the Dalai Lama and more than 100,000 of his people to flee to India and Nepal. The Red Army proceeded to carry out Beijing's policy, but the so-called modernization of Tibet and conversion of its people to Communism turned into genocide. The decade of the Cultural Revolution, incited by Mao Tsetung, carried that policy to the extreme. In addition to systematic looting and removal of Tibet's treasures, the Red Guards destroyed over 6,000 monasteries and temples, numerous libraries, sacred artifacts, and rare manuscripts. Approximately 1.2 million Tibetans lost their lives. The country's natural resources were senselessly plundered, causing extensive damage to ecology and environment.

During the 1980s, after a short-lived liberalization, Deng Xiaoping offered Tibet as the sacrificial lamb to the radical members of the Politburo. The final aims turned out to be complete colonization and sinofication. The dramatic events of the spring and summer of 1989 in Tiananmen Square have given an indication of the monstrous suppression Tibet has had to endure for decades.

To sum up China's destructive policy in Tibet, I quote from the report of the International Commission of Jurists, based in Geneva: "...the most pernicious crime that any individual or nation can be accused of, viz. a willful attempt to annihilate an entire people."

More than one hundred thousand Tibetan refugees, mostly peasants, have been resettled in India, Nepal, and Bhutan. They are making a tremendous effort to preserve their religion and culture in an unfamiliar environment. The revival and expansion of Tibetan Buddhism has been impressive, thanks in large measure to the education of the children. Today, in exile, Tibetans continue to follow with reverence the wise and compassionate leadership of His Holiness the fourteenth Dalai Lama.

2 Contemporary Tibet: Cultural Genocide in Progress

Anne Klein

[China's rule in Tibet is] ''more brutal and inhumane than any other communist regime in the world.''—*Alexander Solzehnitsyn, October 9, 1982*

''We don't have one hair's worth of freedom.''
                        —*Tibetan pilgrim at the Potala, October 3, 1988*

Background: 1950-1980

Since the dawn of its recorded history in the seventh century, religion has suffused every aspect of Tibetan culture. Through four centuries (seventh to eleventh) of contact with Indian Buddhism, the great Tibetan temples and monastic universities became repositories for indigenous Tibetan statuary, paintings, and above all, the well-tended libraries that preserved one of the most prolific religious literatures the world has ever known. During the Cultural Revolution, over six thousand of these monasteries were destroyed at Han Chinese instigation, and more than half of the Tibetan historic, philosophic and biographic literature was burned.

The People's Republic of China (PRC) took control and, for the first time in recorded history, Tibetans were labeled a "minority."

This destruction of monastic and other religious life did not occur in a vacuum. On October 7, 1950, the Chinese army invaded the eastern Tibetan province of Kham. While much of world attention was focused on the Korean War, the Chinese army, with full air and artillery support, massacred tens of thousands of Tibetan civilians in Kham. At that time, Tibet was demonstrably an independent state, in fact and in law; it soon became the largest territory to be robbed of its sovereignty since World War II. In May 1951, a seventeen-point agreement was drawn up, absorbing Tibet into the PRC. The Tibetan Delegation summoned to Beijing to discuss this "agreement" was prohibited by the PRC from contacting the Dalai Lama or the Tibetan government as would have been appropriate under international protocol. The papers were thus signed under duress. Although this document was framed entirely by the PRC's problematic claim that Tibetans are one of the nationalities of China, it promised not to alter "the existing political system in Tibet" and stated further that "the policy of freedom of religious belief...shall be carried out."

In 1959 there were an estimated 200,000 monks in Tibet out of a total population of nearly seven million. Following the Chinese occupation of Central Tibet, the entire clergy, and especially the highly revered reincarnated lamas, were singled out by the Chinese for mistreatment. Public execution and torture were commonplace. Monks and nuns, vowed to celibacy by choice, were forced at gunpoint to perform sexual acts in public; others were locked in a room to starve to death and told to "see if your God will provide you with food." Tens of thousands were imprisoned or placed in hard-labor camps throughout Tibet, China, and Inner Mongolia. The majority of these perished or went into exile, and current restrictions on religious education in Tibet ensures that their ranks cannot be replenished.

China's leaders have apologized for the excesses of the Cultural Revolution. At the same time, they continued to maintain that Tibetans welcomed and have benefited from Han intervention. For example, *Highlights of Tibetan History*, written by two researchers at the Central Institute of Nationalities in Beijing, describes the early occupation of Tibet.

Ganden Monastery, Tibet. Photo: Carole Elchert

In August, 1951, the P.L.A. [People's Liberation Army] launched an epic march on Tibet for its peaceful liberation. . . .Wherever they were billeted they helped the local population do all kinds of jobs, took care of their needs and interests and the army medics attended to their sick free of charge. Such good deeds won the hearts of the Tibetans.[1]

In fact, however, over one million Tibetans, one-sixth of the entire population, died as a direct result of the Chinese occupation. They died while fighting, during imprisonments, and from the rigors of escape and exile. They also starved to death during the first famine in Tibetan history, the result of Han insistence that wheat, rather than the traditional barley, be sown in the fields.

Nevertheless, a subtle but crucial obstacle to Sino-Tibetan negotiations today is a very real Han Chinese perception that they are helping the Tibetan people by modernization. The strength of this conviction cannot be overestimated. The Chinese point to new roads, new medical facilities, and electricity as evidence of progress. Tibetans see these as primarily benefiting the Han Chinese who are sent to Tibet as part of a policy of population transfer. They perceive the Han, therefore, as obstructing Tibetan access to the benefits of modernization, rather than as bequeathers of it. Tibetans outside Tibet, moreover, are aware that "modernization" has also meant the installation of seventeen secret radar stations, fourteen military airfields, five missile bases, at least eight ICBMs, and the reported use of Tibet as a dumping ground for nuclear waste.

Equally problematic to Sino-Tibetan communication is the conviction among even the most educated, cultured Han Chinese that Tibetan religious life and culture are a liability not worth preserving. This perception, combined with the presumed benefits of modernization, means that Tibetan discontent is often incomprehensible to the Han. A university professor from Beijing, visiting Tibet for the first time in the 1980s, expressed genuine surprise at the Tibetans' animosity for the Han people living there.

Reversals: 1980-1988

In 1980 China formally repudiated much of its earlier treatment of Tibetans and other "minorities." Officially, these people were free to preserve their own customs and habits.

When the PRC speaks of religious freedom in Tibet, it points, above all, to several monasteries which have been rebuilt since 1980, and to places where pilgrims have again been allowed to prostrate and make traditional offerings of butter. Tibetans themselves note that the local government controls who and how many new monks may enter these monasteries. Once admitted to a monastery, student monks find that qualified teachers are rare, and because monks must take outside jobs and attend to tourists, time to study is the exception. Since 1987, moreover, many monks have been imprisoned in the aftermath of demonstrations in which some of them participated; party officials have permitted no new entrants since that time. For those who remain, studies have been further disrupted for lengthy periods by "confessional meetings" held daily by local Com-

Houses and Jokhang Temple, Old Lhasa, Tibet. Ink Drawing—Philip Sugden

munist cadres. These "meetings" often result in beating and other forms of harassment.

Tibetans lament the impossibility of the dawn-to-dusk study, debate, and training in the ritual arts that were the traditional focus of monastic life. The thirst for religious learning is still so great, and the prospects for gaining it in Tibet so dim, that since 1979 at least 1,600 monks have set out for India and Nepal to study at refugee monasteries. Their search does not always end happily. In October 1988, twenty-seven monks from Ganden Monastery were turned back at the border by Nepalese officials.

The rebuilding of the monasteries signifies very different things to the Han and the Tibetan people. For the Han, it is a symbol of religious freedom and their own benevolence. For the Tibetans, it is a step in the right direction and, at the same time, turns monasteries, which are part of the living culture, into museums. The rebuilt monasteries are located primarily in Lhasa and other areas attractive to tourists. These travellers must buy tickets to enter and are charged as much as five dollars for the privilege of taking pictures in each of many anterooms. The monks are required by law to demand such payment, but often are pained to collect it. In Tibet, custom dictates that everything associated with religious life and arts, from the building of monasteries to the printing of books, proceeds only by donation. It is not unusual for visiting tourists to hear an impromptu apology while fees are collected. Yet, only about a fourth of these monies remain with the monastery; the rest is at the discretion of the PRC government officials.

Since the fall of 1987 there have been about two dozen demonstrations in central Tibet. The PRC has characterized these protests as the activities of a few "splittists" spurred on by the "Dalai clique." In PRC newspaper articles and press releases of this period, Tibetan cultural autonomy is often equated with a return to "feudalism." However, Tibetan refugee communities in India and elsewhere have adopted modern political, educational, and material conventions, while at the same time maintaining their cultural heritage. For them, modernity neither signifies nor requires the demise of Tibetan culture.

On June 15, 1988, the Dalai Lama addressed members of the European Parliament in Strasbourg. He reaffirmed his Five-Point Peace Plan, which calls for the

Destroyed Fresco, Central Tibet.   Photo: Philip Sugden

conversion of Tibet into a zone of peace, so that Tibet can assume what is arguably its traditional role as a buffer between India and China. The Peace Plan also calls for respect for human rights and democratic ideals, environmental protection, and a halt to nuclear dumping and the Chinese population transfer into Tibet. Finally, it seeks earnest negotiations between Tibetans and the Chinese.

In this proposal, the Dalai Lama for the first time did not call for the political independence of Tibet. Rather, he suggested that Tibet become a self-governing and democratic state that is not politically separated from the People's Republic of China. By "Tibet" he means the traditional three provinces of U-Tsang, Kham, and Amdo. Although all three remain culturally Tibetan, as they have been for more than a dozen centuries, only U-Tsang is today included in the "Tibetan Autonomous Region." Kham and Amdo, approximately two-thirds of the traditional Tibetan land mass, are simply regarded as parts of China's eastern provinces—Qinghai, Gansu, Sichuan, and Yunnan.

Tibet and Tiananmen Square

On March 8, 1989, martial law was declared in Tibet. This decree followed three days of riots during which Tibetans attacked Chinese-owned stores and government offices, the first time their antagonism had been vented on the Han community at large. The Tibetan riots were, in part, a response to the gunning down of unarmed demonstrators by Han security forces in Lhasa.

Two months after these events, martial law was declared in Beijing. It has been suggested that the decision to impose martial law in Tibet was a dress-rehearsal for handling civil unrest throughout China. Moreover, in both cities, an apparent tolerance for the initial demonstrations encouraged more persons to become involved. In both Lhasa and Beijing, the subsequent brutal responses took many by surprise. These harsh reprisals were followed by an ongoing roundup of those who had joined the demonstrators, however briefly.

Eyewitnesses have reported that in Tibet mass executions took place under martial law: one hospital morgue housed eighteen Tibetan bodies, eight shot through the side of the side of the head, two through the front, and the others with a "bullet to the back of the head" typical of the Cultural Revolution. Asia Watch and Amnesty International have accumulated evidence of continuing torture in Tibet. Hundreds of Tibetans have been arrested, some taken forcibly from their homes. Torture is still routinely used in interrogation sessions. Before martial law was declared, torture was often used to gain information and to extract "confessions," insofar as the PRC still sought to legitimize its actions through ideology, and to use ideology as means of social control. Since martial law has been in effect, these efforts have ceased, and torture is simply an instrument of terror.

Such are the circumstances of individuals living in Tibet. Tibetan culture as a whole faces additional grave difficulties. The forced influx of Han people into Tibet is perhaps the largest single threat to Tibetan identity. PRC officials deny the existence of such a policy. Whereas there were virtually no ethnic Chinese or Han peoples living in the Tibetan cultural area prior to 1959, Hans today outnumber Tibetans in the Lhasa Valley seven to one. In *The Poverty of Plenty*[2], Wang Xiaoqiang and Bai Nangeng propose that new towns be built from scratch in Tibet and populated by Han migrants with an intact and transplanted social structure.

The overwhelming of their culture by sheer numbers is what Tibetans fear most. It has already happened to other ''minorities'' in the PRC, most notably the Manchurians who now number two million among seventy-five million newly arrived Han peoples in their cultural area. Indeed, the current situation is framed by some Han intelligentsia as an extended phase in a long historical process during which, as a scholar from Beijing's Central Institute of Nationalities expressed it, ''minorities will amalgamate and disappear.'' According to this scholar, compulsory amalgamation, while ''counter-popular,'' is the natural culmination of the current process.

Amidst the intensifying sense of danger to Tibet, the Dalai Lama continues to call for a peaceful response. After being nominated for the Nobel Peace Prize in three consecutive years, he became a Nobel laureate in 1989. On learning of the award, he noted that ''Tibetans today are facing the real possibility of elimination as a people and a nation. The Government of the People's Republic of China is practicing a form of genocide by relocating millions of Chinese settlers into Tibet. I ask that this massive population transfer be stopped.''

The Dalai Lama has lent his support to the democracy movement in China since its inception. In the spring of 1989, he issued a statement in support of it, and after June 4, he mourned the loss of life in Tiananmen Square and elsewhere in the PRC. In responding to his Nobel Prize, he observed that ''The Chinese students have given me great hope for the future of China and Tibet. I feel that their movement follows the tradition of Mahatma Gandhi's *ahimsa* or non-violence. . .the eventual success of all people seeking a more tolerant atmosphere must derive from a commitment to counter hatred and violence with patience.'' In some quarters, a sense of common cause is growing between Tibetan refugees and pro-democracy Chinese living overseas.

Despite expressed willingness on both sides, meaningful top-level discussions between the PRC and Tibetan representatives have yet to take place. Most recently, the PRC protested the Dalai Lama's Peace Prize, calling it an attempt to undermine ''the unity of the nation'' and a ''gross interference in China's internal affairs.'' The Chinese Ambassador to Norway, Li Baocheng, left the Nobel ceremony as the Dalai Lama arrived. In his speech on the occasion, the Dalai Lama said that the Chinese rejection of his 1987 Five-Point Plan was forcing him to rethink his approach, and that he might withdraw that proposal. But, he added, "our struggle must remain non-violent and free of hatred."

As this volume goes to press, the threat to Tibet continues, and the future of reforms in China remains an urgent question. At the same time, numerous members of the U.S. Congress and Senate are actively seeking human rights for Tibet. Bills have been introduced which link trade relations with China with human rights. Organizations calling themselves "Friends of Tibet" are active in several U.S. cities. In these groups, Americans work with Tibetans to publicize the situation in Tibet, circulate petitions, or organize letter-writing campaigns to U.S. Congressmen and Senators. Many of these efforts are being coordinated by the International Campaign for Tibet and the Office of Tibet in New York.

Maintaining tight control of Tibet is costly to the PRC in financial and moral terms. Both the PRC and Tibetans have much to gain from successful negotiations. Although persons on both sides recognize the importance of such talks, the mutual suspicion and differences of perception have thus far forestalled any real progress. But such negotiations remain the only hope for both parties. In the words of the Dalai Lama,

> We must seek change through dialogue and trust. It is my heartfelt prayer that Tibet's plight may be resolved in such a manner that once again my country, the Roof of the World, may serve as a sanctuary of peace and a resource of spiritual inspiration at the heart of Asia.

Notes

1. Wang Furen and Suo Wenqing, *Highlights of Tibetan History*, translated by Xu Jian (Beijing: New World Press, 1984), p.178.

2. Wang Xiaoqiang and Bai Nangeng, *The Poverty of Plenty* (New York: Macmillan, 1989).

Suggested Readings and Contacts

Avedon, John. *In Exile from the Land of Snows* (New York: Vintage Books, 1986).

Gyatso, Tenzin, H.H. the Dalai Lama XIV. *Kindness, Clarity, and Insight* (Ithaca: Snow Lion Publications, 1984).

International Campaign for Tibet, 1511 K St. NW, Suite 739, Washington D.C. 20005. Tel. 202-628-4123.

Shakabpa, Tsepon W.D. *Tibet: A Political History* (New York: Potala Publications, 1984).

Snellgrove, David and Richardson, Hugh. *A Cultural History of Tibet* (Boulder: Prajna Press, 1980).

Tibet Press Watch, 1511 K St. NW, Suite 739, Washington D.C. 20005.

Office of Tibet, 107 E. 31st St., New York, NY 10016. Tel. 212-213-5010.

Tsurphu Monastery, Tibet. Watercolor—John Westmore

3 Ethnic Variation and Cultures of Tibet

Lopsang Geleg and Nancy E. Levine

In traditional Tibetan cultural geography, Tibet is conventionally divided into three regions: West Tibet, T'o Ngari Korsum; Bar-Tsang Ru Zhi, including the Central Tibetan cities and valleys of Lhasa, Yarlung, Shigatse, and Gyantse; and East Tibet, Mad Do Kham Kang Trug. In Eastern Tibet, the traditional regions of Kham and Amdo are now partially incorporated in mainland China's Qinghai, Sichuan, Gansu, and Yunnan provinces.

Some writers have argued that despite the political fragmentation of Tibet through most of its history, Tibetans should be considered a single ethnic or national group. They share a basic culture, a common historical tradition, a common language, and a common religion. Nonetheless, obvious differences exist among people living in different parts of Tibet. There is a striking contrast between settled agriculturalists (*rongpa*) and pastoral nomads, (*drogpa*). Within both these peoples there is substantial regional cultural diversity. Cross-cutting this regional diversity are differences in political organization. Thus, whether a group lived under the central government, belonged to a small chiefdom, or remained wholly independent from centralized control had a major impact on certain features of social life. Visitors to Tibet observe the obvious cultural diversity visibly manifest in features of dress, hair style, language, and interpersonal interactions. Observable regional differences occur in religious practice, as in the cults of local gods; family organization; and marriage practices, as in the differing importance of fraternal polyandry, the well-known Tibetan marriage system which links several brothers to a single wife.

Western Tibet

When dividing Tibet by its conventional regions, one can begin with Western Tibet. This region is historically important; because of its location, it was subject to influences from India, the Middle East, and Central Asia. The principal distinction between its peoples is the contrast between drogpa and rongpa. The nomadic tribes exhibit more cultural uniformity than the villagers, and one manifestation of this is the great diversity in Tibetan dialects spoken by these agriculturalists. Because Western Tibet is high altitude and arid, the bulk of the population is nomadic. Only along the few river valleys can one find low-lying warm places suited for cultivation. Some of the older literature suggests that polyandry was particularly common in the west of Tibet and that this was associated with large household size.

Central Tibet

The next geographical region is Central Tibet, which includes many agricultural villages along the Tsangpo River and relatively fewer drogpa than in the west. The land is lower in altitude, and the climate is damp and mild, suitable for growing highland barley, wheat, corn, broad beans, rice, and rape. These agricultural areas are densely settled, particularly in the rich basin lands of the Yarlung Valley.

Central Tibet was the central place for politics, economics, religion, and culture. Most of the major monasteries were located here. Most nobles lived here, and the famous estates were situated in the rich agricultural valleys. Daily life was organized around those estates held by incarnate lamas, monasteries, and lay aristocrats. These lands and land held directly by the government were farmed by subject peasants hereditarily tied to the land. Peasants were socially categorized according to their rights over parcels of land and their corresponding tax and corvée (labor service) obligations. They lived in villages of varying size with hereditary headmen in some villages and elected officials in others; they had collective rights over forests and pastures. For the peasants, their major social ties were with kinspeople; clanship was not recognized.

While considerable polyandry was evident among certain categories of peasants and among the aristocrats in former times, it is very rare today. In the past, some rationales for polyandry in wealthier peasant families were a concern with excessive family growth and high numbers of dependents to support, the risk of dividing the family property among contending brothers, and the consequent loss of social standing. Aristocrats wished to retain shared rights in their official position, which would be lost if they left the family. The number of brothers linked in a polyandrous marriage was limited, however, due to practices of sending sons to the monastery and occasional invitations for brothers to wed heiresses without brothers.

As the focal point of traditional Tibetan economy, the estates themselves generally occupied an entire valley and were essentially economically self-sufficient. This economy was not monetarily based: taxes were paid in goods and labor. Nobles' profits from their estates were realized entirely in commodities like food and butter; the government paid officials similarly with goods. Because traditional agriculture was not productive enough, people engaged in additional economic activities. Different regions became famed for their different handicrafts. Gyantse, for example, was known for carpet making. Shigatse was famous for its woolen fabric.

This situation changed radically in 1959 when the Chinese instituted socialist land reforms. The traditional estate system was abolished, and the land was distributed equally among individual households. People formed cooperatives, in which they held individual rights over land and engaged in exchanges of mutual aid. Communes were established after the Cultural Revolution. All the land and most domestic animals belonged to the collective, and people worked for points. Following the harvest, the points were totalled, but people received much the same food, whether they were working well or not. As a result, people did not work very hard, and production declined. After 1980, all land was distributed to individual households according to the number of household members, and

Nomad Mother and Daughter, Lhasa.   Photo: Philip Sugden

people were able to cultivate for themselves.

Within Central Tibet, the city of Lhasa has been an important center for Tibetans from all regions. The city has always been a place of higher learning, where many lamas come to study further and to obtain advanced credentials. Many remain and still live there today. Now young people also come to study at Tibet University. Craftsmen and artisans similarly have always been attracted by the opportunities in Lhasa; they have occasionally married Lhasa women and made the city their permanent home. Lhasa has long been a market center, too, where nomads bring butter, skins, cheese, and sheep from the north to exchange for agricultural products and where long-distance traders bring goods from China and India. Traders from as far as Chamdo and Yunnan married and set up families there. Today in Barkhor street one can see people from all over Tibet in their different dress, speaking different dialects, selling and exchanging goods. Finally, people from all over Tibet come to Lhasa for pilgrimage. In all these ways Lhasa remains the window on Tibetan culture.

As for regional distinctions in social life, Central Tibet was known for the plethora of customs signfying hierarchy and respect, as in the use of systems of honorific language (special pronouns, nouns, and verbs to show respect for a high ranking person being described and addressed). This is far less common elsewhere in Tibet, such as in Amdo and Kham.

Eastern Tibet: Amdo and Kham

Another region is Eastern Tibet, which is occupied by various groups of pastoral nomads, among whom the most famous may be the Golog of Amdo. They are famous partly for their independence—even the Tibetan government could not control this region—and for their fierceness, their unity in conflicts, and the threat they posed to traders who passed through their territory. Like other Tibetan pastoral societies, the Golog have a complex socio-political organization which unites thousands of households and widely separated encampments into tribes. Each tribe has rights over a certain territory of grazing land. Each is internally subdivided into smaller tribal units and, within them, into encampments of co-resident households (*rukhor*). Each tribe also has a hereditary line of chiefs who arrange the annual migration, while the tribal segments (*tsho-ba*) have elected leaders.

As with other nomadic pastoralist groups in Tibet, Golog place great emphasis on the worship of ancient mountain gods who have been assimilated into the Buddhist pantheon. The gods are appealed to before any important action is inititated, with recitations of prayers, offerings of butter lamps, music, and gunfire around the mountain. Each tribe has its own special mountain god, but one god belongs to all Golog. Two or three Golog tribes usually join together to maintain a small Buddhist monastery. These institutions, although small, nonetheless serve as centers of culture, education and religion, and as markets. People gather there on religious holidays, and old people no longer able to travel with the herds live in the monastery precincts.

Another important cultural region in Eastern Tibet, though distinct from Amdo, is Kham. The Washu Serthar of Kham are another group of nomadic pastoralists

Tenzing Darkay, Choglamsar. Graphite Drawing—Philip Sugden

who occupy the rich lands that now lie between Qinghai and Sichuan. They form an alliance of forty-eight separate tribes, each with well-defined rights to certain sectors of grassland. All members of a given tribe hold equal rights in the land; the pasture and encampment (*rukhor*) is reassigned annually, either by rotation or the casting of lots. Among the Washu Serthar, the sense of territorial rights is very strong: young people patrol the grassland, and incursions from other tribes' animals may lead to skirmishes and to casualties.

The households which form an encampment make four camps annually. These seasonal encampments are staggered like four flights of stairs along the various altitudes of the occupied valley and generally consist of three- to five-tent households. Members of the households include close relatives and some unrelated people. The latter households are linked by their complementary economic imbalances: some families are rich in livestock but poor in labor, while others have an excess of workers but an insufficient number of animals to support themselves. The poorer households then work for the wealthier ones, although the two cooperate as equals in other collective activities.

Washu Serthar include three inner tribes, descendants of the three brothers who first settled the area. Members of this clan also have moved among the other tribes. Thus they link different tribes, providing a point of unity in tribal structure. Only men of this clan can serve as chiefs. Tribal chiefs organize the military; settle disputes, including blood feuds; and organize annual festivals focused on the tribes' various mountain gods. Since the area has very few monasteries, people often depend on the aid of spirit mediums or *lhapa* to foretell the future.

Tibetans speak of the fearlessness and roughness of Washu Serthar. Like the Golog, they take pride in displaying individual courage by martial activities and raiding. Tibetans draw a firm distinction between robbery as part of a raid or retaliatory strike and theft from fellow tribe members or people under the tribe's protection. The losses of men in fighting created a surplus of women in this group, even before the rebellion against the Chinese. Many women, therefore, never marry; they spend their lives in their parental tent. If they have children, they expect only a few animals and occasional aid from the child's father. Due to the non-marriage of women and cultural traditions, the families are frequently extended laterally—between siblings—and generationally—including sometimes great-grandparents and great-grandchildren.

Like the agriculturalists, pastoralists underwent many changes after socialist reforms were instituted. They were organized into cooperatives, collectives, and then communes, the last involving work in production teams. As occurred with the agriculturalists, productivity declined. During the Cultural Revolution, people began to wander about because their earnings each year were so low. In 1979-80 animals were distributed to individual households according to family size. The

Tibetan Layperson Chanting.
Charcoal Drawing—John Westmore

collective also lent animals to the poorer households, and the production teams were disbanded. Finally, fixed prices for sales were abolished, and people now are free to sell their products either to the state or on the open market. Before 1959, the socio-political circumstances of these Eastern tribes, the Golog and Washu Serthar, differed markedly from that of pastoralists living on the Chang Tang, or northern plain, of Western Tibet. Western tribes were ruled by the central government in Lhasa; many were the subjects of noble or religious estates. For administrative purposes, many of these tribes were linked together by the Lhasa government, but the government also subdivided tribes in order to assign different segments to different estates.

Eastern Tibet's geography is also distinctive. In Eastern Tibet, the mountains and rivers run from north to south instead of west to east, as elsewhere in Tibet and China. Because of the terrain—mountains cut by valleys—many people live a half-agricultural, half-pastoral life. They keep houses and farms in the low valleys and raise yak and sheep in the high pastures near their villages.

Southern Kham has a very good climate for agriculture. For example, Bathang cultivates two crops a year and produces many fruits and vegetables. Bathang is one area that has long been close to ethnic Han Chinese influence; it also was exposed to Christian missionaries in the past. These are often advanced as reasons for the absence of polyandry. In Bathang, however, a system of clanship not found among the agriculturalists of Central and Western Tibet evolved.

Other areas of Kham were formed into independent kingdoms, like the five Hor principalities. Most of the land then belonged to the kings and nobles, to whom peasants owed corvée labor. Unlike in Bathang, polyandry was highly esteemed and in certain districts was extremely common. Polyandry also was economically advantageous, in that it permitted brothers to specialize in different types of work. One brother would trade, while another herded yak and sheep, and the third cultivated the family's land. These Horpa were famous traders who transported Chinese clothing, silk, and porcelain to Tibet and Tibetan wool and salt to India or Nepal, returning with pearls and jewels to trade in China.

To the south and east of Kham lies Minyag, an area which has been Tibetanized. People speak another language at home, but know Tibetan and have become Buddhists. There are distinctive religious beliefs and customs, some of which have been altered due to Tibetan influence. Minyag also is famous for its craftsmen. It is said that people from this region aided in the building of Lhasa before 1000 C.E.

Gyalrong, yet another region east of Kham, consisted of eighteen kingdoms, most with distinctive local dialects difficult for other Tibetans to understand. Gyalrong is now a part of Sichuan province. In the past, warfare was endemic, so people situated their villages atop the mountains (where they suffered a scarcity of water) and built watchtowers which can be found throughout Gyalrong today. The houses also display the effects of this history of warfare. The first floor is very small, while the sides of the second floor extend over the first. Thus the house is difficult to scale because of the overhang. Food is stored in the house—again for self-defense. In the eighteenth century, the Manchu Qing dynasty finally conquered the area and established settlements in the lower valleys along the riverbanks.

Many other areas of Tibet, like Dagpo, Kongpo, and Nyang, are culturally distinctive. We have only touched on what is known about the diversity of Tibetan culture and ethnicity, and these subjects have just begun to be fully described. Much work remains for ethnographers and students of Tibetan society.

Amdo Nomad Woman, Rorgai, Tibet.   Photo: Carole Elchert

4 The Domestic Life of a Town Dweller

Molly McGinn

Lifestyles in the capital city of Lhasa provide both the exception and the rule to lifestyles of the town dwellers throughout Tibet. To the extent that Lhasa, meaning "place of gods," is where Tibetans from distant regions journey on pilgrimage, it is exceptional. More than other towns, its residents have access to goods, services, and information from throughout the country and from beyond the borders. Yet, despite foreign tourists, a mixed population influx, and constant pilgrimage activities, the daily life of the Lhasa resident depicts a fundamental pattern that repeats itself throughout the towns and villages of Tibet.

A Day in a Tibetan Life: Daybreak in the Home

Even before the early morning light ignites the distant peaks, the roving dogs of Lhasa announce the daybreak. Wisps of smoke from the morning cooking fires begin to rise and hang above the awakening town. As the towering golden roofs of the Potala Palace, home of the exiled Dalai Lama, catch the rising sun, in a nearby home, Ama-la (literally, a polite form of the word *Mother*) crawls out from under the yak wool blankets of her brightly painted bed.

Cooking Tsampa, Rorgai, Tibet.   Photo: Carole Elchert

At fifty-eight, the widow Ama-la has lived in Lhasa all her life. In another bed sleeps a grown son and two young nephews. She has two rooms for the seven to nine members of the household; another son and his new wife live in the other room. She shares her bed with an elderly aunt who has lived with the family as a housekeeper since before any of Ama-la's five children can remember.

The room is rectangular with brightly painted pillars that run up to the center of the ceiling and support the adobe, mud-brick construction. The floor is packed earth. On the coldest nights in the winter, the room is heated by a wood burning stove. Wood is expensive, however, and Tibetans generally tend to cope with the cold by wearing extra layers of thick clothing and going to bed early. Despite the altitude, the daylight hours even in the middle of winter are sunny and pleasant.

Ama-la's son, who is a carpenter, has furnished her rooms with yellow and blue flowered chests and drawers, one topped with a Buddhist altar. The Dalai Lama's photo is near the center of the altar, next to a statue of the Buddha. Every morning Ama-la puts on a black wrap-around wool dress called a *chuba*, winds her two long braids around her head, puts fresh water in the silver altar bowls, burns incense, and chants a prayer. In towns all over Tibet, the morning smells of incense.

Family Life

The elderly aunt is busy stirring the coals and rekindling the fire. The family's adobe brick oven stands in the cooking alcove. Many families among town dwellers have additional unmarried women helpers in the household. Sometimes the helper is a second wife, a situation more likely if she and the first wife are sisters. In some areas of Tibet among the nomads, two or more brothers will share a wife. Pairs sharing a spouse will often be siblings.

Young people are guided by, but not confined to, their parents' wishes when it comes to choosing a spouse. Teenagers are generally shy and the slightest hint of interest in the opposite sex causes waves of gossip. Attending the local film as a couple becomes the equivalent of announcing an engagement. Often, one son will bring his bride to live in his parents' home. When a child is born, a lama gives the child a name and a red blessing string to wear around the neck.

The Preparation of Tea and Food

Ama-la pumps water into the kettle to make the butter tea that abates the morning cold. She and her courtyard neighbors share a well, but many people must take their clothes, bicycles, blankets, and even trucks to the river for washing. Once the tea leaves are boiled, the dark liquid is poured through a strainer into a tall wooden butter churn. Ama-la adds a fist-sized lump of yak butter and three pinches of salt, and she churns for several minutes. The steaming frothy brew is kept hot in a Chinese thermos and drunk throughout the day. For Ama-la, as for most Tibetans, this tea is the primary source of fat in this high, dry land. Unlike the children, Ama-la and the other adults prefer eating *tsampa*, the tradi-

House at Nargatse, Tibet.   Pastel Drawing—John Westmore

tional mainstay of roasted barley flour moistened with butter tea and kneaded into a paste.

Beginning the Day

As the rest of the family awakens to the smell of the fire and the plunging sound of tea churning, the road which encircles the Central Cathedral ten minutes away is already alive with a stream of circumambulating and prostrating devotees. For these nomads, the journey to Lhasa is a form of prayer through which they obtain merit and a chance for a better rebirth. It is through this slow-moving, mantra-droning procession of pilgrims that Ama-la's young nephews will find their way to school.

After a breakfast of steamed bread and tea, they grab their book bags, sling their wooden Tibetan alphabet boards over their shoulders, and leave for school. Although the children study Tibetan script and grammar and speak Tibetan at home, the medium for all other subjects is Chinese. Children all over Tibet read and write Chinese better than Tibetan. Older people struggle with spoken Chinese; most neither read nor write Chinese and many cannot write Tibetan either.

A Day's Work

Ama-la's working children give her part of their pay to buy supplies every month. In Lhasa, most people work in shops, small carpet factories, or in offices. Outside of town, and in smaller towns, most people grow barley and raise a few head of livestock. The high altitude and severe daily temperature differential limit cultivation to all but the hardiest strains of barley. Women are just as likely as men to be seen doing difficult manual labor or managing shops. Middle- and upper-level management and political positions are primarily held by men; whereas women are equally represented among physicians.

Few individuals own cars, but most companies, schools, and service organizations have their own trucks or cars. Wages vary greatly from fifty or sixty yuan to several hundred yuan a month (US$20-$150). Chinese workers who come from outlying provinces receive—as high altitude compensation—nearly twice the normal wages they receive at home in China proper.

Ama-la walks to the open market to buy yak milk yogurt, butter, and whatever vegetables are available. She always buys a supply of the neighbor's homemade barley beer, the *chang* Tibetans serve their visitors. Some money is set aside every month for donations to the monks of Ganden Monastery. The remainder of an average day is filled with cleaning, sewing, cooking, and visiting with the neighbors.

Medical Emergencies

Traditionally, the study, collecting, and dispensing of herbs for Tibetan medicine was done mostly by monks. Now, the larger towns have clinics for Chinese,

House at Shalu, Tibet.   Ink Drawing—Philip Sugden

Western, and Tibetan medicine. When Ama-la has trouble with her teeth, she goes to the Chinese dental clinic. For her recurring nightmares, however, she goes to the Tibetan clinic. At the Tibetan clinic, treatment includes the physician's casting the patient's horoscope. Treatment at the Chinese medical clinic includes pulse diagnosis as well as the standard Western examination procedures.

Social Activities: Evenings and Special Occasions

Whenever friends gather at Ama-la's house on any given day, the chang flows liberally. The success of a wedding party is judged by the number of people that get very drunk and dance. Long hat pins are held menacingly close to the ribs of those who are not drinking enough.

Festival days for the full moon, or the lunar new year celebrations, are filled with preparation of special foods, decorations, and nights full of bonfires. On these days in particular, people circumambulate the Central Temple. Especially at the new year, there is drinking and eating at Ama-la's home, and all the children and their children gather to celebrate. Her distant sons, away from home during the new year, ache with homesickness for the warmth, laughter, and spiritual richness that is uniquely found at home in Tibet.

Today: Style and Lifestyle

For hundreds of years the lifestyles of the Tibetans underwent little change because of their country's relative isolation. Today, the residents of Lhasa watch themselves on the world news. Diffusion of education, technology, and political forces insure that change is constant in the few major towns. However, those same influences have little effect on the outlying villages. In Lhasa, this divergence is strikingly evidenced by a daily spectacle: Sheepskin-clad teenage nomads with sun- and grime-darkened faces curiously inspect their city cousins who strut in Levi's and down jackets—both groups converging and intertwining in the traditional clockwise procession around the Central Cathedral.

Sakya, Tibet.   Photo: Carole Elchert

5 Domestic Life of Nomads

Gary Wintz

Wanderers on the Roof of the World

Over the years I have spent living and traveling in Tibet, my most remarkable experiences have been with the nomads of the great Tibetan Plateau. These pastoralists who roam the rugged and remote regions of our earth's rooftop live in a world that is in many ways suspended in time in a medieval period.

In the extreme northwestern corner of Tibet's high plateau there may still be nomadic herdsmen who have yet to see the four walls of a building or, for that matter, their first Communist official. Seemingly untouched for two thousand years, small, scattered clans of herders wander with their tents and tend their yaks, sheep and goats. To nomads their livestock represent living sources of their only considerable wealth.

Extraordinary Endurance

In a land of extreme continental climate where a blistering sun can alternate with a snow blizzard during the course of a day, the nomad's endurance is legendary.

Tibetan Shepherdess, Ladakh.   Photo: Philip Sugden

It is said that a custom among some Tibetan nomads is to leave a newborn baby unattended outside the tent its first night. If still alive by next morning, the baby is considered a "keeper."

The romantic image of these herdsmen as unfettered is shattered by the realities in most areas of a "liberated" and "modern day" Tibet. In fact, the majority of Tibetan pastoralists today are within at least a few days' journey of a Chinese-constructed road. Access to roads makes it possible to "export" their valuable products of milk, cheese, meat, and wool to free markets in valley towns where they must meet government-enforced quotas.

Bureaucratic Feudalism

The arm of socialist bureaucracy can be a long one, and today new tensions are arising from government edicts that demand the decimation of herds as the offi-

Nomadic Encampment, Chang Tang, Tibet.   Pastel Drawing—John Westmore

cial response to overgrazing. The program that forced communalization of the nomads during the Cultural Revolution was a tragic failure and was abandoned—hopefully forever. It is too early to know if the new government's attempts to corral these independent-minded wanderers will succeed. By the very nature of their lifestyle, Tibet's nomads still enjoy a degree of freedom in following their traditional patterns of living. This relative freedom to follow old ways is the envy of their fellow countrymen—agriculturalists and townspeople alike.

Although the intensive Chinese immigration onto the plateau has also produced some new Han yak herders in Amdo and Kham, most Han Chinese work as merchants and officials in the towns. The nomads still have most of the vast upland

Nomad Camp, Chang Tang, Tibet.   Ink Drawing—Philip Sugden

grasslands to themselves. Much of their daily material culture is unaffected by the massive sinofication occurring in cities and villages.

Nomadic Tent Life

A visit to a nomad's home—a woven yak-haired tent—is like stepping back a millenium. Were it not for the metal bands around the wooden butter churn, the metal cooking pot, and perhaps even a color Dalai Lama photo, the scene could almost be Neolithic: A huge pile of dried dung patties is stacked in one corner; yak cheese dries on a string over the dung fire; and yak butter wrapped in animal skin sits in another corner. Wooden spindles and piles of sheep wool divulge the crafted origins of the heavy blanket bedrolls.

An extended family sleeps through the long bitterly-cold nights, pooling body warmth in the close proximity of a small room-size tent. On a winter day, the black yak hair of the roof soaks up the sun's intense rays and makes the tent warm enough for infants to play naked. Outside the tent during a blustery flurry, I have seen hardy nomad women milking the herds with their chubas thrown open so that snowflakes landed and melted on their bare shoulders.

During the day the grandmother or another adult watches over the infants and the tent and keeps the tea brewing. Meanwhile, the older children and other women tend to the milking and feeding of herds tethered around the camp. A clan campsite usually includes a few extended families within calling distance of each other. The men pasture the other flocks and herds on slopes and the steep sides of distant ravines. They chant Buddhist mantras and spin wool as they roam—with a rock sling handy to keep strays in check.

The Dream of His Holiness's Return

Despite the allure of TV and disco, most nomads are unattracted to the controlled life in villages and cities. Pilgrimages to the few remaining temples, however, are now somewhat tolerated by the atheist authorities. So many nomads, all of whom are deeply religious and follow His Holiness the Dalai Lama, occasionally wander to the holy city of Lhasa. They bear gifts of valuable yak butter for the monasteries, where they pray for the long life and hopeful return of their most revered spiritual leader.

6 *Unity and Diversity in a Religious Tradition*

Marilyn R. Waldman

Most of us take the existence of religion so much for granted that we forget it was created by modern scholars so that they could study it.[1] To be sure, human beings do say and do things that can be considered religious, but to imagine a single entity called religion requires us to make an artificial separation among certain dimensions of human experience. The grammar of the situation is significant. Using the adjective, religious, reminds us that we are talking about one dimension of human life that is interrelated to all the others, but using the noun, religion, implies the existence of a separate thing with a life of its own. This language usage also promotes an artificial distinction between religion and culture (another creation of modern scholars) and often leads people to think that culture infringes on the purity of religion, or allows people to explain unacceptable religious practices as belonging to culture rather than religion.

The same can be said about the various things we call religions or religious traditions. The suffix *-ism* comes so naturally to contemporary speakers of English that it allows them to organize easily a variety of things into an entity that seems very real indeed. Thus, we speak of Judaism, Buddhism, Hinduism, Taoism, Confucianism, Zoroastrianism, Jainism, and Bahaism. Another major reli-

Nyingma Monks, Lhasa.   Photo: Carole Elchert

gious tradition is now generally called Islam in English, but Islam was first and
for a long time known in English as Mohammedanism until non-Muslim scholars bowed to Muslim sensibilities about the way that term distorts their faith.
The term Christianity, which uses another suffix in English (though not in French,
where it is styled *christianisme*), is something of an exception. Unlike the -ism
religions, Christianity is used, not only for the religious system per se, but for
the body of Christians and for the state of being Christian. Still, it construes many
separate things as a single entity.

This division of religion in general into proper-name religions in particular makes
the whole of each separate religion seem more real than its parts. It also tends
to promote a monolithic treatment of the whole. To be specific, an explanation
of why there is diversity is more important than proof that there is unity to begin
with, and we are required to relate the parts to the whole more than to each other. Thus when we feel the need to talk about Buddhism as opposed to various
Buddhisms (or Buddhist traditions) and to explain and sometimes justify the relationship of one to the other, we are trying to solve a problem that we are largely

responsible for creating. That is why Wilfred Cantwell Smith has urged us to talk not about Buddhism, but rather about Buddhists; not about Christianity, but about Christians, and so forth.[2] As in the distinction between *religion* and *religious,* the use of qualifying adjectives to describe certain clusters of attributes reminds us of the variation from person to person, group to group, place to place, and time to time.

Insiders to particular sets of teachings also have their own ways of explaining and labeling variation among themselves, but they do not always use an umbrella word of their own that describes a single thing with many parts. Some groups describe their own way as the way and other ways as less correct or less authentic than their own, or even as unacceptable, that is, what is called heterodox or heretical. Others might distinguish between the true way, as summarized in certain canonical texts, and the mere customs that have come to be associated with their faith, often mistakenly, in particular locales. Others take a more open view, as in the Indian story of the human being who was given truth to carry in the form of a huge mirror. Finding it too heavy, or stumbling, or both, the human being drops the mirror, which shatters into a million pieces. Everyone who comes by picks up a piece, sees truth in it, and mistakenly thinks he or she possesses the whole truth. But the wise observer knows that each piece is but a reflection of the whole.

All these insider and outsider approaches combine to produce many ways of conceptualizing the relationship among the various parts of the wholes to which we have given single names: as the cord that holds a string of (graduated) pearls together; as a tree with many branches off a single trunk; as a single central stem with offshoots or, worse, suckers; as a shrub whose roots are common but whose branches separate and diverge at the point of origin; as slices of a pie; or as pieces of a puzzle. And just as some of these views celebrate diversity, others aim to reduce it.

The choice of approach(es) is particularly important for a study of Buddhism, which, like Christianity, is one of the world's most variegated and segmented religious traditions. Many aspects of Buddhism's history have contributed to its variety. One of them, a strong missionizing impulse, is not unique to Buddhism. It is shared by other traditions, such as Islam and Christianity, which have also

Pilgrim at the Jokhang Temple, Lhasa.   Watercolor—John Westmore

spread far beyond their place of origin into a variety of cultural settings. Many Buddhists attribute this desire for expansion to the Buddha himself. Certainly in his own lifetime, the Buddha's disciples had already begun to spread his teachings. By 400 B.C.E., Buddhism had spread to Nepal; by 200 B.C.E., to Kashmir, Sri Lanka, and Central Asia; by the birth of Jesus, to China; by 400 C.E., to Java, Sumatra, and Japan; by 600 C.E., to Tibet; by 700 C.E., to Thailand, just as Islam was spreading outside of Arabia into North Africa and West Asia; by 800 C.E., to Burma; by 1600, to Mongolia. Since 1800, Buddhism has been spreading to Europe and the Americas.

In two other respects, however, Buddhism is unusual. First, it is the only world religion that has possessed multiple sacred languages since its early centuries—including Pali, Sanskrit, Chinese, and Tibetan—and independent canons (bodies of accepted sacred writings) in all of these languages. According to the Pali Canon, the Buddha instructed all his monks to become missionaries and to spread his word in the languages of the people they visited, far or near. In ancient India this meant using vernacular variants of the Buddha's own dialect, but it could apply to any situation, however far-flung.[3] Characteristically in the history of religions, fragmentation and variation of belief and practice are associated with the use of vernacular languages for sacred writings and their study. A well-known example is the increased denominationalism of Christianity after the Protestant Reformation and the translation of the Bible from Latin, hitherto the Church's only sacred language, into many languages understood by ordinary people. Furthermore, even though the various Buddhist Canons overlap and share many points, no single collection of Buddha's sayings and teachings is used by all or comes directly from him, even though his words are an important source of *dharma*. And the earliest biographies of his life date from several hundred years after his death.

Second, Buddhism, through its emphasis on *sangha*, makes an unusually strong distinction between monks/nuns and laity and involves an unusually large number of people in the clerical life. Furthermore, among the laity religio-cultural practices vary significantly from city to town to village to farm.

In practice, then, a distinction between religion and culture is not easy to make, especially if a religion is not to be defined solely in terms of its most articulate learned written expressions. First, no matter how universal a religious idea, it cannot be expressed universally; it must find expression in a locally meaningful form. Second, certain customs are felt and practiced as a sincere part of piety, even if they cannot be documented in the written sources of a religious tradition. And third, certain "folk" customs thought to be unrelated to a tradition's written texts can often be shown to be connected with them in surprising and complex ways.

So if one asks whether such-and-such really is Buddhism, the answer depends on one's point of view. Any humanistic study begins by taking seriously the subjective understanding of those who identify themselves as Buddhists or as adherents of any other faith. At the same time, the values, negative and positive, that various insiders have assigned to these differences through time and space must be discovered and understood.

It is always possible, of course, for a point of view to change, whether it be-

Monk at Labrang, Tibet.   Photo: Carole Elchert

longs to an insider or an outsider. Mahinda Deegalle, a Theravada Buddhist monk from Sri Lanka, was chosen to deliver the Baccalaureate sermon at his 1989 graduation from Harvard Divinity School. In his address Deegalle reflected on how his encounter with American religious pluralism had broadened his understanding of his own religious tradition:[4]

> Because of my experience at Harvard I am able to see Buddhism as a pan-cultural religion by going beyond my own Theravada Buddhist perspective. At Harvard I have met living representatives of various Buddhist traditions. This has caused me to think of Buddhism in a different light.

He then identified tolerance for religious diversity as a key attribute not only of Buddhism, but of the Buddha himself:

> Buddhism has always confronted the challenges of pluralism. Buddhism originated in India in the middle of diverse religious traditions. When Buddhism spread throughout Asia it had to embrace a wide range of cultures and traditions. So I think it would benefit us all if we see what the Buddha taught about pluralism. The Buddha advocated the importance of freedom to choose one's own religion.

One can only hope that the increasingly frequent interreligious encounters of the contemporary world will continue to broaden our understanding of diversity within and among traditions, as it did for Mahinda Deegalle.

Notes

1. Jonathan Z. Smith, *Imagining Religion From Babylon to Jonestown* (Chicago and London: The University of Chicago Press, 1982).

2. Wilfred Cantwell Smith, *The Faith of Other Men* (New York: New American Library, 1965).

3. Richard H. Robinson and Willard L. Johnson, *The Buddhist Religion: A Historical Introduction* (Third Edition; Belmont, CA: Wadsworth Publishing Company, 1982), p. 109. For an excellent account of the development of early Buddhism and its expansion into Tibet, see Chapters 3 and 9.

4. Mahinda Deegalle, ''Baccalaureate Address 1989,'' *Harvard Divinity Bulletin* (Summer 1989).

7 Buddhism and Christianity: An Internal Dialog

Claude Philippe d'Estrée

When asked to compare Buddhism and Christianity, I am forced to look internally and listen to the dialog I have had with myself for more than twenty years. All of us who are practising Buddhists in the West belong to one lineage or another. (A lineage is the "denomination" of our particular form of Buddhism.) For some practitioners, a Zen Roshi traces their teachers to Japan and the abbots of a specific monastery or a Tibetan lama whose incarnations have been reborn for hundreds of years. Or perhaps we simply trace our lineage to a Buddhist school of thought in Cambodia, Thailand, India, Korea, or China.

So, while we are Buddhists, we are also American-Japanese Buddhists or American-Tibetan Buddhists. We inherit the baggage of the culture along with the teachings of the masters.

But we also have another lineage, that of the religion of our birth. So we are also Methodist-Buddhists, Reform Jewish-Buddhists, Roman Catholic-Buddhists, Sunni Islamic-Buddhists. In many families our cultural heritage is taken very seriously—Swedish-American, German-American, Mexican-American, and so on—and is thrown into the pot as well. So here I am, a first-generation American of French and Russian parents, baptized in the Russian Orthodox Church, educated in parochial schools by the Jesuits of the Roman Catholic Church, and practicing the teachings of the Madyamika School of Tibetan Buddhism. Being an American-Franco-Russo-Orthodox-Catholic-Tibetan Buddhist is sometimes a very confusing state of affairs.

But let's reduce the discussion to something more manageable. I am a Christian-Buddhist. Those of us born and raised in the Christian Church will, in some form or other, always be Christian-Buddhists. When I try to explain Buddhism, I have to first run it through the sieve of Christianity. I use the language of the Church and the language of Western psychology to make clear the message of Buddhism. When I try to understand Buddhism for myself, when I try to internalize the teachings, I again have to run it through the sieve of Christian theology and Christian culture. Hence the internal dialog.

Can the two religions be compared? When a Buddhist takes refuge in the Buddha, the Dharma, and the Sangha, how much of that can be understood by comparing it to the salvation found in Christ, the Scriptures, and the Church? Is meditation or sitting practice for the Buddhist the same as Christian prayer? Does the Russian icon perform the same function as the Tibetan thangka? Before I compare these two great traditions and show their similarities, I should make clear that there are also major differences between the two. And while it is important to notice what Buddhism and Christianity have in common, it is also important to note and even celebrate the differences that make each unique.

For many years I tried being a Buddhist and a Christian at the same time, practicing both equally. I was inspired by a meeting between the celebrated writer and Trappist monk, Thomas Merton, and His Holiness the Dalai Lama. They spoke at length about their respective religions and their spiritual practices and found little or nothing about which to disagree. Who was I to argue with such wisdom? It took me years to realize, with the help of another wise teacher of mine, Krister Stendahl, that they were reaching from the depth of their own tradition to the depth of the other.

It has been argued that all religious traditions are simply different paths up the same mountain and that somehow all the paths meet at the top. I am no longer

White Tara, Collection of His Holiness The Dalai Lama.   Photo: Philip Sugden

convinced of this. Perhaps each tradition is an arduous path up different mountains. When we reach the peak, the moon may look very much the same and the valleys and plains below similar, but each is seen from a different perspective. It is also impossible to be on two mountaintops at the same time. With that in mind let us briefly look at these two traditions.

The central characters in both religions are compelling individuals. Both were born in ancient lands and equally ancient cultures. While Sakyamuni Buddha was born a wealthy prince and Jesus Christ a poor carpenter's son, we should remember that Jesus was nonetheless born in the direct line of the House of David. Though born five hundred years apart, they were both born into religious traditions that had become rigid with the letter of the law. These two teachers encountered a caste system that was prescribed and proscribed from the priestly caste down. They encountered a religious system based on a person's socioeconomic class at birth, the dietary restrictions followed, the clothing worn, the money spent at the temple, and the prayers chanted aloud. In their cultures, then, the religious system seemed more concerned with the outward appearance of religious belief. Into this system, both teachers came to reform. They broke down the elite caste barriers and opened spiritual life to everyone. They insisted on the spirit of the law while respecting and reinterpreting the letter of the law. They understood that the "internal appearance," that is, the internal spiritual health of the individual, was central to religious life. And they brought to the world two central themes, love and compassion. These two radical ideas cut through all the baggage of class, race, politics, and gender. These two religious principles, that if practiced to their fullest, could change the face of humanity and human nature and assure us of the highest spiritual potential.

When we take refuge in the Buddha, we are acknowledging a human being, no different than ourselves, who struggled with the questions of birth, old age, sickness, and death. After much discipline and personal deprivation, he found a path of spirituality between too little and too much of those two things. Buddha discovered that grasping and attachment of the material and immaterial world causes most suffering. Like a physician, he suggested a cure, the Eight-Fold Path, which, when followed, would not only make us healthier and happier but would allow us to also treat others. The Buddha, the Awakened One, showed us how

Cauldrons at Sera Je Monastery, Tibet.   Ink Drawing—Philip Sugden

to find the buddha in ourselves, the great potential of which we are all capable. He showed how to become truly awake to ourselves and the world around us.

If my Christian upbringing colors my Buddhism, then Buddhism, in turn, helps me reinterpret Christianity. Jesus then becomes the example of how to live in the world. He was a rebel and a rabbi. He brought God to humanity so that women and men could become closer to God. He found the prostitute, beggar, and the tax collector preferable company to kings, princes, and priests. He healed the blind and the lame and raised the dead from their eternal sleep. He threw the money changer from the temple and walked upon the stormy sea to challenge our faith. He was in this world but not of it, and for his daring and revolution of the spirit, he was crucified like a common criminal. To make sure no chain that bound our minds and hearts was left unbroken, he himself rose from the dead, walked among those he knew and loved, and ascended bodily into heaven. When Christ was tempted by the Devil, and the Buddha by Mara, they both turned down the material riches of this world and chose the far more difficult path of leading a humble, spiritual life in this world. The reward is enlightenment and heaven. These treasures make gold and worldly power pale in significance.

We know of the lives of these teachers because their words were written down by their followers. It is significant to note that they themselves did not keep a diary of their meetings with people, the stories they told, or the truths they propounded. They wrote no sermons nor published any theological or philosophical tomes. What we have is the recollected account of their words written down sometimes hundreds of years after the fact. What is miraculous is our knowing instinctively that what was written accurately rendered, for the most part, what was actually spoken.

The Buddha asked that we treat his words like a goldsmith treats gold—testing, heating, and hammering to make sure the words are true gold. We can test both the Sutras and Scripture. We can take refuge in their truths. Taking refuge in the Dharma means, in part, taking refuge in the sutras of Sakyamuni Buddha, but it is more than that. It implies taking refuge in the order of the universe and knowing there is coherence in the seeming chaos of the world. It implies knowing there is a path which you and I can follow with the help of all the great Buddhist teachers and commentators who followed in the footsteps of the historical Buddha.

When I look at Scripture, I see a grand plan, a history of God's people, the rise and fall and rise again of kings and prophets, and the interaction of God with humanity. While the Buddhist canon may seem much larger than the official canon of Christianity, there are no spare words in either. Each story has a purpose; each line can stir us to action or thought. Scripture and Sutra are like onions. Peeling away layer after layer of meaning can reveal new meaning, new insight, more truth.

I find it fascinating that both Jesus and Gautama spoke in parables, stories that teach—perhaps the language of prophets and teachers. They used parables to spark our imagination and to get our slow wits moving. They used them to explain the the kingdom of heaven, the reason for evil in the world, the universal aspect of death, or the existence of God. These gems of wisdom may be what we remember most. Having a staying power that defies explanation, parables are passed on from generation to generation of believers with wonder, amusement, confusion, and awe. They are often difficult to understand and not always comforting because the truth is not always very comfortable. We know, however, that their inspiration is completely human and yet completely divine.

We also collectively see and interpret the teachings of Buddhism and Christianity through the Sangha and the Church. Taking refuge in the Sangha originally meant taking refuge in the monks and nuns who practiced Buddha's teachings full time. The Sangha were revered for their discipline and wisdom. They made the sacrifice of home and hearth, and to them went the reward of *nirvana* (enlightenment). Now, the Sangha not only includes monks and nuns but all the practitioners of *buddha-dharma* (truth or teachings). We don't have to be at the top of the mountain to help another. Receiving some guidance from someone who has already made it past that boulder in the path or worked out the toe-holds in the apparently sheer rock before us may be all we need.

But Buddhism is also a solitary path. We, in a very real sense, are our own masters. The struggle and the effort are our own; we reap the rewards or suffer the consequences of our actions. While Buddhist practitioners do gather for ritual and ceremony, the "hard stuff"—the sitting practice, the meditation—is done alone. In the West we have modified this process, and I am convinced that the modification is a direct response to the gathering in church and synagogue. Western Buddhists meditate together in shrines, halls, homes, and classrooms. We are drawn to form a community. We are inspired by the Church as a community of believers who come together to share in prayer and worship in faith. Sundays are a time to hear the Word, partake in the Divine Liturgy, and converse during the coffee hour that follows. It is no mistake that the time in which we share in the breaking of bread and the drinking of wine, which represents the body and blood of Christ, is called Communion because we commune with Christ and each other. From this community of faith called the Church, we draw strength, courage, and wisdom; the Church binds one to the other. The monks and nuns of both traditions may be seen as the flower or the root of their faith, and the Sangha and Church would be greatly diminished without them, but it is all people of the Sangha and the Church who bring the teachings alive and make them living faiths.

While it is true that we understand the world with our minds, it is also true that we first perceive the world with our eyes. Thus the visual impact of religious symbols lays the foundation for the subconscious understanding of the meaning of our faith. It is this vision of Christian and Buddhist symbols (icons) that bridges the outer world with the inner reality.

> The visible world was made to correspond to the world invisible and there
> is nothing in this world but is a symbol of something in that other world.
> —Abu Hamid Muhammad al-Ghazzali, *Ihya*

When I was a child and attended Easter service in the Russian Orthodox Church, I was always drawn to the icons. The Easter service was late at night, and the church was lit by candles held by the congregation and votive candles in front of the icons and the Iconostasis. The priest chanted and the choir responded in low, rumbling, melodious tones. The deacons swung, in cadence, the great censers billowing their blue smoke of incense. The church was often hot and stuffy, and the service incredibly long and boring, especially to a seven-year-old. I tried to get to the side of the church to find an icon, a painting depicting Christ, the church fathers, or one of the saints. But when I was really lucky I found an icon of the Theotokos, the Mother of God with the Christ Child in her arms. Often the painting was a copy of the Vladimir Mother of God, the most holy icon of Russia. Then I was happy, for I could look for hours at her face, her eyes, and his response to her. The three of us rested in quiet conversation until the service with its otherworldly sounds and smells came to an end.

Tsogshing (Merit Field), Thangka at Tibet House, New Delhi.
Photo: Philip Sugden

I grew up with these icons and they still hold a special place on the eastern wall of my home. Now, I sit and meditate in front of thangkas, paintings depicting the Buddha, Bodhisattvas, lamas and yoginis, and Taras. And once again I can sit in quiet conversation for hours.

Thangkas and icons may hang on my wall but they are not art, though great artists have painted them, and some have even been canonized for their artistry. Instead, thangkas and icons are windows into heaven. They transcend the color, the shapes, and the brush; and I am transcended with them. They are symbols in the Greek sense of the word—that which makes present. The icon and thangka combine the two realities of heaven and earth, of the ultimate and the conventional. One reality is not surrogate to the other. The painter interprets these realities for us. The mouth, eyes, ears, nose, hands, and feet need not be anatomically correct because they have been transformed into divine sight, divine touch, divine hearing. The nimbus or halo of Christ or the Buddha seems to emanate as a light source from within the figure. The colors, each its own symbol, radiate with spiritual intensity. Each hand gesture of Christ and each *mudra* of the Buddha has meaning; each object they hold teaches.

The iconogapher thus infuses his art with prayer and meditation from the first choice of cloth or wood to the final rubbing. The act of painting becomes a devotion, a private liturgy. And what does the icon painter leave for last, but the face and the eyes. John Stuart speaks of the painter investing ''the face with the unique 'pneuma'—the spirit and life/force of the saint depicted.'' The icon becomes alive, and the eyes with their incredible depth are sublime because they have seen the Truth. We sit quietly in front of the thangka or icon and listen. They are like royalty, and we wait to be spoken to. And if we are quiet enough, we will hear their voices.

Kipling was wrong. East is East and West is West, but they do meet. Being an American Buddhist and being a Christian Buddhist is not the same as being a Japanese, Tibetan, or Cambodian Buddhist. All these forms of Buddhism are unique, strange, and invigorating. The challenges are great in practicing a philosophy that was born and bred in a foreign culture. How does this philosophy translate to a modern Western industrial culture? How do you practice ''right livelihood'' and be a lawyer, an advertising executive, or a secretary in a multi-

Altar at Samye Monastery, Tibet.   Watercolor—John Westmore

national corporation? How do you practice being a nun or monk in a culture that does not support you? Where does the meditation hall end and social responsibility begin? How do you live with shortsighted environmental, economic, or foreign policy when you are taught to look at the very long view?

One fascinating possibility is that Buddhism serves the needs of the particular gestalt of Asian culture, and Christianity serves the needs of the particular gestalt of Western culture. Tamra Pearson, a social psychologist at Harvard University, and I have had long discussions on this very idea. Generally speaking, Buddhism is a philosophy of the individual. Buddhism interacted with and helped balance a collective society. Christianity, on the other hand, is a religion of community. It has interacted with and balanced a society that highly prizes individualism. What happens, then, when an individualist philosophy (Buddhism) encounters an individualistic society? What may be produced from this merger is extreme narcissism and alienation from the concerns and needs of society.

The Buddha spoke to his culture. Can he speak to mine? I think yes. The alternative to narcissisim is a concern for all sentient beings. Western culture has treated the Earth as its servant with humans acting as lords and masters over all they survey. Mountains are to be defeated, land subjugated, animals domesticated and destroyed. We were given dominion over the earth. But now that thinking must pass. Buddhism posits that all sentient beings are like sisters and brothers and should be treated with the same respect, love, and compassion we confer on our own mother. The earth is alive, and we should live with it in harmony and balance, taking as little as we need and giving back something in return.

My socially active Buddhism can, in turn, be informed by the Christian ideal of sacrifice for one another. I am familiar with the iconography of the West. But can I learn a whole new iconography to truly understand the symbols of thangkas? And if I can break through the cultural baggage of Buddhism, its teachings may shed new light on my own culture. I may be able to see with new eyes and hear with new ears the problems and possibilities of Western and, in particular, American culture and society. This allows the possibility of new solutions. Let me give you one possible example. My childhood religion of Christianity becomes alive again, for the more I try to understand the universal teachings of the Buddha, the more I encounter the universality of Christ's teachings. I then can begin speaking from the depth of one tradition to the depth of the other.

8 *The Experience of Buddhism*

Lotsawa Tenzin Dorjee

Many journalists and interested people have enquired about the philosophical and spiritual underpinning of Tibetan nationalism. What role does Tibetan Buddhism play in Tibetan nationalism? This is especially pertinent when we consider that the recent demonstrations in Tibet were spearheaded by Buddhist monks or what the press chose to term as "the warrior monks."

Partly in answer to those questions and for the benefit of readers who wish to obtain a clear picture of the broad principles and tenets of Buddhism, *Tibetan Bulletin* has requested Venerable Tenzin Dorjee, a translator at the Library of Tibetan Works and Archives, to present his view of what Buddhism is.

Compassion as the Base

It has been more than 2500 years since Lord Buddha came to the world to share his transcendental experiences. In order to guide people along the path to enlightenment, he taught numerous doctrines based on compassion and the scientific attitude. The principle of non-violence blossomed from his great compassion.

Buddha did not dogmatically impose particular views but taught everything compassionately to suit people's inclinations, interests, mental caliber, etc. For those inclined toward a simple path (Hinayana), he taught detachment; for those inclined toward a more extensive path (Mahayana), he taught the Bodhisattva perfections—generosity, morality, patience, enthusiastic perseverance, concentration and wisdom. For others inclined toward the most profound path (Vajrayana), he taught the esoteric vehicle that utilizes attachment. In Buddhism, then, the three vehicles appeal to a person's disposition to be a Hearer, a Solitary Realizer, or a Bodhisattva.

The Scientific Attitude as the Base

Buddha did not want people to follow him blindly, but rather to do so using their intelligence. He unambiguously stated: "O Bhikshus and wise men! Just as a goldsmith examines well his gold through burning, cutting and rubbing it, so should you accept my word. But do not accept it merely out of respect for me." The objective study of the facts, as important in Buddhism as in science, is a striking parallel between them.

The four reliances traditionally explained in Buddhism are important to note. These four are: do not rely on how the teacher looks externally while listening to teaching but rely on what he says; do not rely on the words so much as on the meaning conveyed by them; do not rely on interpretative meaning but rely on the definitive meaning; finally, do not rely on the sense consciousness but rely on mental consciousness during meditation.

Relevance Today

Some people mistakenly think of Buddhism as a religion of the past. In fact, Buddhism is a timeless message, one that is still useful today. His Holiness the Dalai Lama has said on many occasions that Buddhism posseses two salient features regarding conduct and view [practice and theory].

As for conduct, Buddhism advocates non-violence, wherein lies the prospect for genuine world peace and harmony. These are issues for which concerned voices are heard from all over the world, and toward which efforts are being made through

Drigung Monastery, Central Tibet.   Photo: Carole Elchert

disarmament talks.

As for Buddhism's view, it involves the philosophy of "dependent arising," an approach essentially in harmony with modern scientific methodology. Dependent arising (reliance upon causes and conditions) touches upon everything in the Buddhist world. Were Buddhism merely based on faith, it would not be able to face the challenge of scientific scrutiny. Scientists and Buddhists are working closely together these days and contributing much to each other.

The Doors to Enter Buddhism and the Great Vehicle

The door by which one enters Buddhism, not academically but practically, is through ultimate refuge in the Three Jewels, which are the Buddha, his doctrine (the *dharma*), and the spiritual community (the *sangha*). Buddhist practices are

Fire Puja, Namche Bazaar, Nepal.   Ink Drawing—John Westmore

based on this refuge. Of course, academic interest in Buddhism has merit; yet without practice, the study of Buddhism becomes like the study of any ordinary subject, such as history and political science. In such a case, one does not gain inner realization. The altruistic mind of highest enlightenment is the door to enter the Great Vehicle (Mahayana). This mind is the noblest attitude in Buddhism and is oriented towards promoting the ultimate welfare of all living beings.

It is in terms of attitude that the distinction is made between the Lesser and the Great Vehicles. The practitioners of the Lesser Vehicles (Hinayana) are primarily concerned with the attainment of personal liberation, whereas those who have adopted the Great Vehicle (Mahayana) are mainly concerned with attainment of supreme enlightenment for the sake of others. This does not mean, however, that the practitioners of the Lesser Vehicle do not work for others at all. Although

Spituk Monastery, Ladakh.   Ink Drawing—Philip Sugden

they themselves do not practice the Great Vehicle doctrine, they sometimes teach the Great Vehicle to others.

Removing Misconceptions

These two vehicles are established in relationship to one another. It is not correct to consider them as factions within Buddhism working against each other. To despise any part of the Buddha's teaching constitutes forsaking the doctrine. An individual training in the graded path fully integrates all the doctrines of the two vehicles. If studied correctly, nothing is inconsistent in Buddha's entire teaching. Rather, the different teachings complement one another.

Schools of Tenets

Buddha developed three wheels of doctrine at Sarnath, Vulture's Peak, and Vaishali. Later on various pioneers individually elucidated the thought of these Dharma Wheels (set of teachings). Thus arose the four schools of tenets: Vaibhasika,

Sautrantika, Chittamatra and Madhyamika. Sub-schools exist within these four. These schools differ from one another largely in terms of how they present the philosophy of final reality. The former two are the lower schools of tenets whereas the latter two are the higher. It should be noted that an understanding of the lower tenets facilitates an understanding of the higher. Thus they should be seen as rungs on a ladder, all of them serving the practitioner to reach the top.

Tibetan Buddhism

Tibetan Buddhism is just a name; the Buddhism of Tibet is in fact merely an extension of the original Buddhism of India. Some people erroneously label it "Lamaism."

Tibet is perhaps the only country in the world today which has preserved a complete form of Buddhism, both in theory and in practice. The *Kangyur* and *Tengyur* preserve 108 volumes of Buddha's original teachings, along with 225 Indian commentarial treatises. Much of what has been lost in Sanskrit is still preserved in the Tibetan, and there is now an effort to restore the original Sanskrit texts from the Tibetan versions. Another distinction within Tibetan Buddhism there is the existence of four major traditions—Nyingma, Kagyu, Sakya and Geluk. Each school is characterized by a different lineage of teachers that results in slightly different emphases in practice.

The spiritual and temporal leader of Tibetans, His Holiness the Dalai Lama, has summed up the essence of Buddhism as follows: "Help others if you can (i.e., the Great Vehicle doctrine). If you cannot do that, at least do not harm others (i.e., the Lesser Vehicle doctrine)."

Originally published in *Tibetan Bulletin*

9 *Mahāyāna Buddhism: Theory and Practice*

Donald S. Lopez, Jr.

Mahāyāna is a Sanskrit word which means "great vehicle." It is the term used to distinguish a movement that arose some four hundred years after the death of the Buddha and flourished in India until around the twelfth century. During these centuries, the followers of the Mahāyāna produced a vast literature, contributed major works to the domains of art, and effected innovations in Buddhist philosophy and practice. Among the factors characteristic of the Mahāyāna are the view of the Buddha as an eternal presence associated physically with reliquaries called *stūpas*, a belief in the existence of myriad Buddhas working in the universe for the benefit of all beings, and an attendant emphasis on the universal possibility of enlightenment for all, monks and laypeople alike.

Perhaps the distinguishing feature of the Mahāyāna is its emphasis on the *bodhisattva*. A bodhisattva is a person who, out of compassion for the world, takes a vow to become a Buddha in order to lead all beings out of suffering to the bliss of enlightenment. The Sanskrit term bodhisattva was translated into Tibetan as *byang chub sems dpa'*, "one who is heroic in his or her aspiration to enlightenment." The path of the bodhisattva is a long one. It encompasses aeons of cultivating such virtues motivated by an extraordinary compassion as giving, ethics,

Monks and Pilgrims at Karma Dupgyo Choeling Monastery, Ladakh.   Photo: Philip Sugden

patience, effort, concentration and wisdom.

A common tenet of Buddhism is that suffering is caused by ignorance. This ignorance is defined as a belief in intrinsic self nature. Mahāyāna philosophy expands upon earlier teachings to see ignorance not simply as a misconception concerning the nature of the person, but a misunderstanding of all things. The mistake is to conceive of things as existing in and of themselves—independently, autonomously, possessed of some intrinsic nature, some inherent existence. Wisdom, then, is the understanding that all things, including persons, are devoid of such a nature, and are, in reality, empty. This doctrine of emptiness (*śūnyatā*) is proclaimed in a genre of Mahāyāna literature known as the Perfection of Wisdom sutras (*prajñāpāramitā*). In order to become enlightened, the bodhisattva must develop both wisdom and compassion fully—must dedicate himself or herself to work forever for the welfare of the other while simultaneously understanding that all beings, oneself and others, do not exist ultimately, that they do not exist as they appear.

Pilgrims at the Jokhang Temple, Lhasa.　　　　Ink Drawing—Philip Sugden

The practice of the Mahāyāna takes essentially two forms, both focused on the bodhisattva. The most influential of the Mahāyāna sūtras, such as the *Lotus Sūtra*, proclaim that all beings will eventually become Buddhas, which means that all will traverse the bodhisattva path. Thus, one form of Mahāyāna belief emphasizes practices for becoming a bodhisattva and performing the bodhisattva's deeds. As bodhisattvas advance along the path, they become increasingly adept at allaying the sufferings of sentient beings, often through magical intercession. Consequently, the other major form of Mahāyāna practice is concerned with devotions intended to procure the aid of these compassionate beings. The bodhisattva Avalokiteśvara is the particular object of such reverence in Tibet, where it is believed that this bodhisattva takes successive human births as the Dalai Lama. Avalokiteśvara is invoked by the famous mantra, *om maṇi padme hūm.*

Mahāyāna Buddhism is the form of Buddhism that flourished in China, Japan, Korea, Tibet, Mongolia, and much of Central Asia. What distinguishes Tibetan Buddhism from the other forms of Mahāyāna Buddhism is the relatively late date of its establishment. While the transmission of Buddhism from India to China took place between the first and eighth centuries, it spread from India to Tibet between the eighth and thirteenth centuries. This late transmission had several important consequences. First, the Tibetans had access to a wealth of commentaries on the Mahāyāna sutras. These works in many cases had little influence in China or were never translated into Chinese. These texts, called *śāstras*, dealt with a range of subjects and included treatises on philosophy, logic, and the structure of the path to enlightenment. Hence, one of the primary differences between East Asian and Tibetan Buddhism was an emphasis on certain sūtras in the former, but an emphasis on the śāstras in the latter. Coming into existence as Indian Buddhism came to a close, Tibetan Buddhism had access to the full range of Indian Buddhist literature.

According to traditional accounts, the Tibetan script was invented for the purpose of translating Buddhist scriptures from the Sanskrit. Scores of Indian *paṇḍitas* were invited to Tibet to aid in the task of translation. As a result, the most complete repository of Indian Buddhist literature is preserved in the Tibetan language, even more than in Sanskrit, since many Sanskrit manuscripts were lost over the centuries. Furthermore, the Tibetan translation of lost Indian texts are considered more accurate than those preserved in Chinese. However, Tibetan contributions to Buddhist thought did not stop at translation and preservation. Making use of the vast literature available to them, Tibetan scholars of all orders made creative syntheses of the Indian materials and produced innovative interpretations of the classical issues of Indian Buddhism.

In the realm of Buddhist practice, the Tibetans were able to witness and assimilate the most important development of late Indian Buddhism, Buddhist *tantra*. Tantra, known also as *vajrayāna* and *mantrayāna*, was considered an esoteric approach to the Mahāyāna path whereby the length of time needed to become a Buddha could be abbreviated from the standard length of three periods of countless aeons to as little as three years and three months. The chief technique for effecting such an extraordinary reduction was an elaborate system of ritual, visualization, and meditation in which the practitioner considered himself or herself to already be fully enlightened with the marvelous body, speech, and mind of a Buddha.

10 *Tibetan Buddhist Monastic and Intellectual Culture*

Robert A. F. Thurman

Since the Chinese occupation of Tibet began in 1950, more than six thousand monasteries and nunneries were systematically destroyed as part of a campaign to ''reform backward thinking'' and ''abolish parasitic institutions.'' In the communist attitude (somewhat like the attitude of the ''protestant ethic'' underlying modern industrialization), the goal of human life is production, work that benefits the people, the collective or whole society. This is the opposite of the attitude of a Buddhist monk or nun, who considers the aim of human life to be freedom and enlightenment and consciously refrains from doing worldly work, being willing to risk death in order to discover the higher life in enlightenment.

The Chinese Communists thus thought they were doing the Tibetans a service by freeing them from enslavement to the monastic institutions, in which some estimate as much as one quarter of the Tibetan population lived, supported by the surplus produced by the other three quarters. They began to destroy the monasteries in Eastern Tibet in the '50s, holding dramatic ''class struggle sessions'' in which peasants were forced to beat, revile, spit on, and kill monks and nuns, in order to overcome the supposed superstitious awe they had been indoctrinated to feel toward these religious persons. They accelerated the destruction in Central and Western Tibet during the '60s and made the devastation appallingly thorough with the Cultural Revolution up to the death of Mao in 1976. The land itself was denuded of Buddhist monuments, as the Communists even went to the trouble of dynamiting *chortens* and shelling cliff-face carvings and paintings of Buddhas and deities. And a whole generation was brought up under Communist indoctrination, free of "monkish oppression and religious education."

We can imagine the surprise of the Chinese in the '80s. After the trial of the Gang of Four and Hu Yao-Bang's visit to Tibet when he acknowledged the disastrous failure of China's policy in Tibet, the Chinese let the Tibetans have some slack to rebuild their economy. Spontaneously, without any central direction or plan, Tibetans began first to rebuild their monasteries all over Tibet. Young men and women—who had never been allowed to own a rosary, to bow before a Buddha image, or to revere a lama, and who knew no religious doctrines, who had memorized the "Little Red Book" and other Marxist-Leninist scriptures— renounced their lay status and sought ordination as celibate monks and nuns. They found old lamas recently released from years of concentration camps and forced labor gangs, and began a course of study, prayer, and meditation to find their way in the *Dharma* (the path revealed by Buddha). In fact, the terrible hardships these young people suffered while growing up made them quadruply intense in their devotion and their practice. Those who found inadequate opportunities in Tibet escaped to India and Nepal to join the free monasteries there. Others made the labor of rebuilding monasteries under the most adverse conditions a part of their practice. Near Lhasa at the famous central monastery of Ganden—completely destroyed in 1966, with the tomb shrine of the national saint, Lama Tsong Khapa (1357-1417) blown apart with dynamite and his mummified body viciously torn apart by ravenous dogs—surviving lamas converged and began a mass civil disobedience by rebuilding as much as they could stone by stone. When the Chinese police arrested one group of workers, others took their places, until the authorities left them to their "reactionary obsession."

The Chinese were utterly astonished that the Tibetans had totally rejected the thirty years of indoctrination. They were amazed that a people in such poverty,

Debate at Labrang Monastery, Tibet.   Photo: Carole Elchert

having gone through years of extreme famine and deprivation, would turn to non-economic pursuits the moment they had some free time. What was this monastic culture of the Tibetans that they prized so dearly? How could a people forced into modernity so earnestly struggle to return to a "medieval, feudal" lifestyle? The Chinese modernity and the Tibetan modernity were radically opposed in their views of freedom and servitude.

To explain this fully takes more space than that available here. The word "monastery" for the Buddhist institution is a bit misplaced, as the Indian *vihara* simply means "abode." The Buddhist monastery was never primarily a place of isolation, as in the case of early Christian monastic communities. It was an alternative community from the beginning. To enter it was considered a liberation in itself, a freedom from social duties to the economy, the family, the tribe or state. "Ordination" is not a good term for initiation into the Buddhist monastic community, as the Sanskrit term *upasampada* means "completion" or "graduation." In Tibet those who could not enter the Order, either because of obligations or because of unwillingness to give up the pleasures of sexuality, family, ownership, and so forth, were delighted that others could enter the Order and eagerly supported local monasteries and nunneries. These monasteries were centers of peace, leisure, education, research in philosophy, psychology, medicine, and arts, and most importantly, producers of happier, more useful human beings. In ancient times, from the point of view of the rich Indian city states and eventually empires, they were internal safety valves wherein dissatisfied and venturesome individuals could pursue their personal highest interests through arduous conquest of self, without engaging in revolutions and external conquests. From the point of view of modern (i.e., post seventeenth-century) Tibetan society, they were voluntary mechanisms of population control, surplus manpower pacification, character reformation, transformation, and positive development.

The monastic institution was not easily accepted in countries outside India such as Tibet where Buddhism spread. It took the warrior Tibetans about two hundred years from the formal introduction of temple and doctrinal Buddhism (ca. 600 C.E.) to build their first monastery at Samye and ordain their first seven experimental monks. A nation of external fighters against enemy armies would naturally resist an institution based on the primacy of the internal fight against the enemy passions, hatreds and delusions. By about 850 C.E., a chauvinistic revolt against the foreign monastic ideal destroyed that first monastery, and the monks had to flee to Khotan and China to save their vocations. From the mid-tenth century until the seventeenth, the monasteries slowly grew in importance and influence, seesawing in the power scales with the warrior aristocracy in the medieval pattern familiar from Europe in those centuries. Finally, in the 1640s, the monastic institutions took the responsibility for governing the whole country. The Great Fifth Dalai Lama developed a completely new form of monastic government, one unique for the planet at a time when the secularization process ushered in by the Reformation in Europe was completely destroying the power of European monasteries.

From the seventeenth century until 1949, the modern Tibetan monastic culture flourished without serious interference or problems. The land was peaceful and secure from most predatory enemies, without the people needing to main-

Stairway at Sakya Monastery, Tibet.   Ink Drawing—Philip Sugden

tain any sort of army. The warrior aristocracy was neatly bureaucratized, working in offices alongside learned monk officials. The economy was well organized and minimalist, sufficiency being the goal rather than infinite economic expansion as in the West. Rich and poor were there, but they were not very far from each other. This loose hierarchy was based on spiritual attainment, which was an infinite horizon open to every single member of Tibetan society though not necessarily taken full advantage of by all. The major portion of the national budget was spent on the support of the monastic universities, which turned out thousands of enlightened teachers of broad erudition and profound insight into the

Debates at Ganden Monastery, Tibet.   Pastel Drawing—John Westmore

human mind and objective reality.

It is key here to realize that Buddhism in Tibet was not really a religion in the sense of a system of beliefs, but rather an educational system developed to cultivate an individual's moral, psychological, and intellectual perfection in the context of an unlimited horizon of human potential. A national medical system was put in place, with the monastic cities each containing hospitals, asylums, and infirmaries. The arts flourished explosively, and there were numerous public celebrations involving sculpture, painting, song and dance, drama, sports festival and epic theatre. Most importantly, the people felt the immanent presence of their divine benefactors: the Bodhisattva Archangels of compassion, Chenrezi (Avalokiteshvara) and Tara, alive among them as their day-to-day leader (the Dalai Lama) and their nurturing mother; the Bodhisattva Archangel of wisdom and intellectual genius, Manjushri, living as numerous reincarnate lama teachers who gave anyone interested in ultimate liberation all the tools of education and contemplative training necessary to reach the highest conceivable goal of actual Buddhahood itself in this very life; and the Bodhisattva Archangel of power, Vajrapani, to keep the negative forces at bay and keep Tibet's cheerful little millennium free from outside interference from the expansionist Chinese, Russians, and British, and from the warlike Gurkhas, Turks, and Mongols.

This unique Tibetan sacred society was based on peace, nonviolence, a postmodern "small-is-beautiful" economy, and the relative equality of the sexes. All individuals had full access to the highest education possible for a human being, that leading to transcendence of suffering and metamorphosis into full enlightenment. This is something quite different from the image brought to mind by the term "medieval" frequently used to describe Tibetan society before the 1950s. That term arises from and suggests the pre-modern European experience of constant warfare, superstitious ignorance, poverty, oppression, and violence surrounding a few fragile monastic islands of peace, learning, and devotion. Instead, the Tibetan Buddhist society was based on what I call an "inner modernity." This attitude—a rational, individualistic quest for the full meaningfulness and fruition of human life through the development of the unlimited powers of the human intelligence, heart, and body—created a spiritual industrial revolution whose factories were monastic universities turning out enlightened human beings.

11 *Cultural and Religious Symbols and Values*

Gary L. Ebersole

As in every traditional culture, the communal values of Tibet find expression in all aspects of life—social, political, economic, aesthetic, and so forth. It is the shared religious worldview or cosmology and religious anthropology (the understanding of the human condition and how this problematic condition might be overcome) which is most important and which informs all of the other dimensions. To a large extent Vajrayana or Mantrayana Buddhism has provided a conceptual umbrella for popular religious practices for over a thousand years, at once offering the promise of protection from negative states of mind and providing a meaningful cognitive structure for living with a higher goal in mind. In this section some of the cultural symbols found in Tibet are introduced, and their religious meaning is indicated.

Some of the most common (and thus conspicuous) religious practices are related to the goal of accumulating spiritual merit (positive attitudes and habits). Tibetan Buddhism assumes the existence of a universal law of causality or cause-and-effect known as karma. This law dictates that every action produces a consequence, but, unlike the physical laws of mechanics, every action has a moral value—positive or negative—attached to it. An act of compassion toward another living being, for instance, has a positive value. Taking of a life, injuring another, or impeding someone's progress on the path to enlightenment, on the other hand, is negatively valued. In practice this belief in karma developed into a sort of spiritual banking system, with the final tally at the end of one's life determining the form and condition of one's consequent rebirth. The ultimate spiritual goal of Tibetan Buddhists is to achieve full enlightenment in order to be of most benifit to others. One finally transcends the cycle of birth-death-rebirth propelled by afflictive emotions (the world of suffering). Buddhists believe that all forms of life are interdependent. Through karmic action, one may be reborn in different form up or down the scale of beings—from hungry ghosts and animals to the gods—though the human form is the most auspicious since it is most conducive to achieving enlightenment.

In addition to generating a highly developed system of morality, the belief in karma has also produced a wide variety of seemingly mechanical means of accumulating merit, which are especially popular among the laity. One of these is the spinning of prayer wheels. Prayer wheels are small hand-held cylinders or huge mechanisms in temples and monasteries. In either case, each revolution of the prayer wheel is believed to accrue the merit of a recitation of the mantras (a powerful sacred formula) contained within the prayer wheel. Mantras such as *Om mani padme hum* (the mantra of the bodhisattva of compassion, Avalokiteshvara) are believed to be a means through which one contemplates the essence of the mantra—in this case, the quality of compassion—and thereby brings into oneself something of that essence. This generation of a beneficial state of mind is considered meritorious. In morphological terms, this practice is similar to the Roman Catholic use of rosary beads, which are also found in Tibetan Buddhism. A related practice for accruing merit is the engraving or painting of the mantra on stones, called mani stones. These are then added to piles by the roadside, at crossroads, or other prominent areas. Anyone travelling in Tibet will see thousands of such stones beside roads and paths. Then, too, "prayer flags" or banners have prayers and mantras written on them. It is believed that as these flutter in the wind, the prayers are carried aloft as offerings. This not only cultivates attitudes of respect and generosity but is also another expression of the belief that the entire universe, animate and inanimate, is interrelated.

The religious activities of lay people are varied, but most commonly the faithful seek to accrue merit by visiting temples, making pilgrimages to sacred sites, repeating the mantras, turning prayer wheels, planting prayer banners, placing mani stones, and contributing funds for the performance of various rites in the temples and monasteries. The monasteries themselves are sacred sites and objects of veneration because they house the *sangha* or clergy, one of the "Three Jewels of Buddhism." The other two are the Buddha and the *dharma* or holy teachings. Moreover, large monasteries are often headed by incarnate lamas who are thought to be the re-embodiment of earlier eminent lamas or even bodhisattvas. The Dalai Lama, for instance, is considered to be an embodiment of Avalokiteshvara. Certain mountains are believed to be the abode of specific deities or are identified with the deities themselves. In addition, innumerable local and regional deities, both male and female, exist. Lay persons light butter lamps or candles and burn juniper or other aromatic plants in order to honor spiritual beings or placate powerful deities of the land in the belief that their prayers are wafted to the heavens along with the smoke.

Some of the basic symbols found in Tibetan life include the mandala, the *stupa*, the *vajra* or thunderbolt, the *phurba* or ritual dagger, the conch shell, the bell, and the drum. Tibetan Buddhism has a highly developed art tradition, including painting, sculpture, and architecture, as well as religio-aesthetic performances. The most common subject portrayed in Tibetan art is the multitude of buddhas and bodhisattvas, famous lamas, peaceful and wrathful meditational deities, and terrifying protector deities. Tibetan art, then, is essentially sacred, religious art. It is not "art for art's sake," but art that serves as a means (*upaya*) to achieving the spiritual goal of enlightenment. Tibetan art was produced and then used in the service of religious practice. The depictions of Buddhist deities do not seek to portray beings with any permanent or real ontological being, but rather symbolize fundamental spiritual qualities such as wisdom and compassion, which together lead to *bodhicitta*, the mind of enlightenment. Similarly, the so-called "terrifying deities" are not understood as demonic in the Western sense, but rather as representing the essential nature of life and cosmic processes, as well as the workings of the human mind. The lama Sumpa Khenpo (1702-1775) expressed the Tibetan perspective on the function of art succinctly: "Since art con-

Pilgrim at Rorgai, Tibet.   Photo: Carole Elchert

sists of body, speech and mind, it must be understood as the harmonious coalescence of all learning.''

The symbolism found in Tibetan art usually expresses the underlying order which informs the phenomenal world and life as we know it. The form of the stupa, for instance, at once symbolizes the structure of the material universe (the Buddhist cosmology) and the path and process of salvation. *Chorten* is the Tibetan word for stupa, and literally means ''heap'' or ''mound.'' Chortens are frequently used as reliquaries to house relics of famous lamas, and thus become objects of veneration as repositories of sacred power. They can be very small, no more than a few inches in height, or massive structures. At the bottom of these forms is a square base representing the four cardinal directions and the earth element. This is surmounted by a dome shape representing the earth element. This in turn is topped with a series of rings (usually ten or thirteen in number) which represent both the Buddhist heavens and the stages of enlightenment as well as the fire element. This is then topped by a symbolic umbrella disc representing the air element. On top of this is a crescent moon, a sun-disc and a flaming drop which represents ether or space.

A mandala is a divine environment which represents the final goal of enlightenment. It is created in the imagination; however, as an aid to meditation, two-dimensional mandalas, which are a sort of blueprint, are depicted in paintings. As is the case with stupas, mandalas both represent the structure of the cosmos and symbolize the order and harmony of an enlightened mind (*bodhicitta*). From within a state of meditation on emptiness, a meditator calls forth in the imagination a celestial mansion or mandala used to evoke deity images. The deities and their meanings are contemplated but also recognized as the meditator's own thought-forms. At the conclusion of the meditation they are then dissolved back into emptiness. The mandala, then, is an instrument by which one integrates spiritual essences, cultivating divine pride combined with clarity and insight.

The two-dimensional painted mandalas seen in temples are blue-prints for constructing these imagined celestial mansions and their resident deities. Although there are many different mandalas, all have a square shape with four walls, four entrance ways, and the main deity of that particular mandala in the center. The center and the four cardinal directions are represented by different colors symbolizing the five primordial wisdoms. Peaceful mandalas are usually surrounded by a circular pattern of rainbow colored light, while the mandalas of wrathful deities are encircled by a ring of fire. Between the circle of fire and the house of the wrathful deity, eight cemeteries are often depicted containing corpses, skeletons, various animals, trees, stupas, etc. Imagining themselves as the central deity, but also understanding their identity with the entire mandala, meditators perform various activities and contemplations, thereby effecting a spiritual integration from the point of the axis mundi. The ultimate goal of employing a mandala in meditative practice is to collapse or overcome all notions of independent self-nature, to realize that the phenomenal world and all beings, divine and human, are dependently originated and are unreal when considered as separate independant entities, but real in essence since they all emanate from the same Buddha nature.

Kumbum Chorten, Tibet.   Ink Drawing—Philip Sugden

This ultimate insight of the *mysterium uno* or the *coincidentia oppositorum* is frequently represented in the form of the sexual union of a buddha or deity with his consort. Known as *yab-yum* in Tibetan, this iconographic image represents perhaps the core insight of Vajrayana Buddhism. However, this sexual imagery, like the various esoteric tantric practices first developed in India, has little to do with sex as the term has come to be used in the modern West. Rather, the imagery suggests the state beyond ecstasy and enstasy (the meditative practice of internalizing the universe as one's own body), that of enlightenment. With enlightenment, all differences—male and female, inner and outer, I and thou, etc.—are integrated.

This same deep meaning is symbolized through other forms as well. For instance, the vajra (literally, thunderbolt), or *dorje* in Tibetan, and hand bell are paired together. These two objects may be held by either a deity or a lama in thangka images (again representing the integration of male and female, wisdom and compassion, or reality and appearance). The typical dorje is a scepter of metal, bone or some other material with five prongs at each end—four at each end curved around a central vertical prong—and collectively representing a five-fold scheme used in mandalas. The dorje represents *upaya*, ''right, fit action,'' which is considered to be a male aspect. When coupled with *prajna* or ''wisdom,'' considered the female aspect and represented by the bell, the result is the mind of enlightenment or bodhicitta. Thus, both the Buddhist path and the ultimate spiritual goal are symbolized in both the yab-yum pose and in the characteristic iconographic pose of a deity holding a dorje in his right hand and a bell in his left. The same meaning is conveyed when, in the course of performing a ritual, a lama or practitioner crosses his or her arms while holding these ritual objects. The vajra is equated with the diamond insofar as it is capable of cutting the bonds of all substances that tie beings to the world of suffering, yet itself cannot be cut. It also expresses that aspect of the Buddha nature which is immutable, pure, radiant, and clear.

Other common symbols found in Tibet are the *phurba* (Sanskrit *kila*; literally, a peg), which is a three-edged ritual dagger having the shape of a tent peg. Its three blades symbolize the power of religion to overcome ignorance, anger and attachment, and it is used in ritual practice to nail down and ''fix'' evil spirits to the earth, thus keeping them from causing havoc and mischief in the world. This belief may not be unrelated to the Eastern European tales of pegs driven through the hearts of vampires to keep them from going abroad in the land.

Other common ritual objects are the conch, drums, and horns of various sorts and sizes. The conch is sometimes used in rituals believed to have power over

Tidrom Nunnery, Tibet.   Pastel Drawing—John Westmore

rain and, thus, the conch is frequently decorated with associated water symbols such as dragons and clouds. Thigh-bone trumpets are also blown by Buddhist priests in a special rite to keep damaging hail storms away from the fields. The hand-drums (*damaru*) found in Tibetan Buddhist practice probably date from pre-Buddhist times. Their use shows the continuing influence of shamanic practice and represents ecstatic flight. The sound of the beaten drums is believed to frighten away evil spirits.

All symbols, then, participate in an encompassing religious world of meaning which can be realized expressly through life in this world.

12 *Tibetan Visual Art*

Barbara Lipton and Nima Dorjee

Introduction

Tibetan visual art is primarily religious art that has a ritual function. Religious statues and paintings (*thangkas*) are revered because they are used as aids to meditation and visualization of the deities, and they have the ability to inspire and motivate the practitioner. It is therefore essential that images be made accurately, according to descriptions written in sacred texts, so that the deity may enter the statue or painting. In this way the art gains merit for the worshipper, for the artist who made it correctly, and for the donor who paid for it.

The subjects of Tibetan works of art can be Sakyamuni Buddha himself, other religious deities, or historical figures such as the Dalai Lamas and other famous lamas and kings. Mandalas representing the dwelling place of the deities, stupas (*chortens* in Tibetan), the reliquary monuments representing the spiritual or truth body of Buddha, and other ritual objects are also made. Objects that are intended to be placed on a shrine or in a temple, as well as articles of daily use, are designed and executed with great skill and artistry. Tibetans, however, do not create art to serve only as attractive decoration, nor do they paint landscapes or

Statues at Spituk Monastery, Ladakh.   Photo: Philip Sugden

still lifes except as background in paintings or wall frescoes having religious or historical content.

Early Buddhist Art according to Western Scholars

Most Western scholars consider the earliest Buddhist art (sixth century B.C.E. to the first century C.E.) to be aniconic, that is, symbolic of Buddha rather than representative of Buddha in human form. These symbols include the *stupa* holding precious relics of and representing the truth body of Buddha, the wheel of the law (*dharmachakra*) representing Buddha's teaching, and the Bodhi tree representing Buddha's enlightenment.

Hundreds of years after Buddha's death, around the first century B.C.E., a new Buddhist movement called Mahayana (the Great Vehicle) arose in India. The

Mahayana taught a path to liberation for all beings through savior figures called Bodhisattvas. Scholars believe that the first figures, or icons, were made after the growth of Mahayana. Early images dating from the first to third centuries C.E. have been found in Mathura, India, and in Gandhara, which is now Pakistan. These early figures were of the historical Buddha, Sakyamuni, but later art also depicted Bodhisattvas and the great pantheon of Buddhist and Tantric deities that evolved.

Eary Buddhist Art according to Tibetan Scholars

The Tibetan version of the beginnings of Buddhist art, however, does not coincide with the generally accepted Western view, and is based on Indian works translated into Tibetan.[1][2] According to Tibetan scholars, paintings and statues of Buddha were made in India in the sixth century B.C.E. during Buddha's lifetime. A painting of Buddha on cloth was said to have been commissioned by King Bimbasara of Magadha in northeastern India as a gift for his friend, King Udayana of Ceylon. The artists painted the picture from Buddha's reflection in the water as he sat by the side of a pool.

Another painting is believed to have been created when Buddha let rays of light from his body shine on a cloth while artists outlined his form. This painting was supposed to have been a gift from Buddha to King Udayana's daughter, the princess of Ceylon. This bodily representation came to be known as *Od-zer-ma*, meaning "taken from the rays."

One of the first statues of Buddha is said to have been a full length, standing sandalwood image commissioned by the King of Gsal-lden (Benares). This statue was based on the King's memory of what Buddha looked like. [According to some sources, King Udayana commissioned the sandalwood image.][3][4] That statue was subsequently taken to China where it was later known as Tsan-dan-gyi Jo-Bo. In 1271, Kublai Khan built a temple to house it in Peking. That temple was destroyed in the Boxer Rebellion in 1900 and the statue disappeared.[5]

Tibetans also claim that there were three statues depicting Buddha at eight, twelve, and twenty-five years of age cast during his lifetime from an alloy of five precious metals (*zichim*) and jewels. These statues were said to represent the "creat-

Marpa Lotsawa, Gold Thangka at Tibet House, New Delhi.
Photo: Philip Sugden

ed body or the body of magic transformation"[6] of Buddha. Tibetans believe that Buddha himself blessed and consecrated these statues by letting rays of light from his body shine on them.

In addition, about eighty years after Buddha's death, three stupas were built, each by one of three brothers from Magadha, in Benares, Rajagri, and Bodhgaya. The temples located beside these stupas were said to contain statues and paintings of Buddha, but all have now disappeared.

Early Buddhist Art in Tibet

The history of Buddhist art in Tibet begins in the seventh century C.E. during the reign of Songtsen Gampo, the thirty-third king of Tibet.

Songtsen Gampo married two Buddhist women: a Nepalese princess, Khritsun (Tibetans call her *Bal-za*, meaning wife from Nepal), and a Chinese princess, Wen-Ch'eng Kung-Chu (Tibetans call her *Gya-za*, meaning wife from China). According to the Tibetan story, the Nepalese princess Bal-za brought to Tibet the statue of Buddha showing him at eight years old. This statue was originally kept in the Jokhang Temple in Lhasa, specially built by Bal-za to house it. The image came to be called Jo-Bo Mi-Bskyod Dorje.

The Chinese princess, Gya-za, spent three years traveling from China through Eastern Tibet to Lhasa for her marriage. She was a sculptress, and on the journey she made stone carvings of Buddha. Two of her freestanding stone sculptures still exist in temples in Kham, East Tibet—one in Minyag Pa Lak-khang and one in Bhum Markham. She is also believed to have made a large rock-carving of Buddha surrounded by eight Bodhisattvas, with Tibetan and Chinese writing carved into the stone, still visible on a mountainside in Rimda, Dagyab, Kham.

Gya-za also brought with her to Tibet another of the early statues of Buddha, showing him as he looked at age twelve. This statue—later called Jo-Bo Sakyamuni, or Jo-Bo Rinpoche—was originally kept in the Ramoche Temple in Lhasa which she had specially built for it. Because of fears of a Chinese attack on Lhasa during the reign of Songtsen Gampo's grandson, the Jo-Bo Sakyamuni was taken from the Ramoche Temple to the Jokhang. It was hidden in the wall of the temple together with the statue of Jo-Bo Mi-Bskyod Dorje (Buddha at eight years old), and a picture of Manjusri was painted over the secret spot. Later, the statues were removed from their hiding place. The Jo-Bo Sakyamuni, showing Buddha as a twelve-year-old, was made the central image of the Jokhang. The other statue of Buddha was then taken from the Jokhang to the Ramoche Temple, thus exchanging their original positions.

In 1959, the Chinese invaders sawed the Ramoche statue of Buddha in two parts and removed the upper section. In 1981, with the permission of the Chinese government, an organized Tibetan committee searched for the statue. It was eventually found on a warehouse porch in Beijing where Tibetan art treasures were melted down. It was united with the statue's lower half in the Ramoche Temple in 1983-84. These two ancient statues of Buddha—the most revered images in Tibet—can be seen today in their temples in Lhasa.

The first statue actually made in Tibet—an eleven-headed Chenrezig or Avalokitesvara, the bodhisattva of compassion—was based on a vision of King Songtsen Gampo. This statue, made of medicinal clay, was originally kept in the Potala Palace and later was moved to the Jokhang Temple where it remained until the Chinese Cultural Revolution. At that time, the Chinese occupiers had it thrown into a sewer. One half of the face was later recovered by Tibetans during the night and was then secretly smuggled to India. It was given to the fourteenth Dalai Lama who was living in exile in Dharamsala. It is now on display in a glass case in the main Tibetan temple, Tsug-lak-khang, in Upper Dharamsala.

Songtsen Gampo also built the first Buddhist temple in Tibet, called Khra-drug, in southern Tibet's Valley of the Kings. In that temple, wall paintings show how his Nepalese queen Bal-za built the Potala Palace and the Jokhang. The Khra-drug Temple was destroyed by the Chinese in 1959 and rebuilt in the 1980s, but the wall paintings are no longer extant.

The Artist's Training

A professional artist creating religious objects can be either a monk or a lay person and should be of high moral character. Frequently an artist comes from a family of artists and spends many years of training with both his own family and other well-known artists. Artists are highly respected for their talent and knowledge and for the study and religious training they have to undergo in order for their object or painting to be ritually correct. They are also trained in art conservation and restoration, since it is the practice in temples and monasteries to keep statues and paintings as close to their original condition as possible to fulfill their religious function. In former times wealthy families kept an artist in residence at their homes where, in addition to a fee, the artist and his family would receive room and board while he worked. At present, unless they are attached to a monastery, artists must support themselves through commissions, sale of their work, and teaching.

Although the description and measurements of a particular subject come from the written scriptures and should therefore be identical no matter who the artist is, in fact artists then and now have leeway in the details and adornments of their work. These details, as well as the refinement and individual talent or skill of the artist, determine the quality of a work of art and make it possible to distinguish one artist's work, or his style of work, from another's.

Tibetan Art Styles

Tibetan art essentially stems from Indian art styles, although sinuous curves are generally less pronounced than in India, and Tibetan art is less sensual despite some overtly sexual portrayals. Strong Chinese and Nepalese influences are also evident, much of the latter having come via metal craftsmen who taught the Tibetans many of their techniques. Regional differences exist between Western, Central, and Eastern Tibetan styles, and schools of paintings emerged that were based upon the work of celebrated individual artists. Styles also varied somewhat throughout different periods of history.

The faces of deities tend to resemble the features of people from the area where the art originates, including Central Tibet, Nepal, Mongolia, China, or India. The appearance of peaceful gods and goddesses were thus based on local ideals of human beauty since people tend to identify most easily with a deity that resembles themselves.

Wheel of Life, Ancient Fresco at Alchi Monastery, Ladakh. Photo: Carole Elchert

Materials and Techniques

In former times giant carvings were made on natural rock while freestanding statues were made of metal or occasionally wood or clay. Today, as in the past, most statues are made from metal alloys. Larger-than-life metal statues are hammered piece by piece, but for the most part images are cast in metal by the lost wax method. Alloys comprised of varying amounts of copper, silver, gold, iron, lead, mercury, tin, zinc or precious stones are poured into molds originally formed of clay. The statues are sometimes cast in several pieces which are then fitted together and often gilded and painted, especially on the face. After a statue is completed, the inside hollow area is filled with prayers, amulets, a life stick, and other riches—an ancient custom called *zung jug*. This practice was expanded upon and celebrated by Lama Buton in the fourteenth century. The object is then consecrated by a lama or high spiritual person with a ritual blessing called *rab-ne* (meaning "stay there") which invites the deity to enter the statue or thangka and remain. The bottom of the statue is then sealed shut with a wooden or metal base usually engraved with the double dorje symbol. As long as that base is intact, the ritual consecration remains with the object. In former times, statues were richly dressed in jewels and in clothes made of silk brocades from Russia, China and Mongolia.

Recent thangkas, like the early ones, are most often painted on sized cotton canvas with water-soluble pigments that come from ground minerals and plants. These pigments, sometimes called stone colors, are then mixed with glue. Thangkas are also occasionally made by embroidery, weaving or appliqué techniques. Before and during the painting process, an artist will chant mantras and appropriate painting instructions that he has memorized. The completed work will also be blessed by a spiritual person. The blessing mantra, *Om Ah Hum,* and the deity's special mantra are written on the reverse of the painting.

Dating Tibetan Art

Tibetan art is created according to ancient written directions specifying proportions, postures, colors, symbols held, and numbers of arms and heads. A work of art may thus be very difficult to date accurately unless an inscription or internal evidence identifies the time period, the artist, or the patron; or unless documentation of provenance indicates where it came from, when it was made, or when it was commissioned. In previous years, objects and paintings were often made by apprentices under the supervision of a master artist, or were made by copying the style of an earlier artist.

In addition, the condition of the object is not always an indication of its age since Tibetans believe in constant repainting, regilding, and restoration of religious art to maintain its ritual function and to show respect to the deity.

Function of Tibetan Art

A practitioner meditating on either statues or paintings tries to visualize the deity appearing before him or tries to visualize himself as the deity depicted, ab-

Altar at Samye Monastery, Tibet.   Ink Drawing—Philip Sugden

sorbing the deity's spiritual energy. The world portrayed in a work of art is considered to be beyond the ordinary world of sense perception and is filled with symbolism and allusion.

Most often Tibetan art is commissioned by a patron, whether for his own home or for a monastery or temple. Art may also be commissioned for funeral ceremonies to insure a better rebirth for the deceased, for recovery from sickness, for guarding against bad influences, or generally for accumulating merit.

Conclusion

Tibetan artists who are working in Asia and in western countries continue to make art for ritual purposes and for sale to collectors. There is also a large market in antique (or sometimes new antique) Himalayan art. Museums that are repositories of Tibetan art are more conscious than ever of their responsibility to preserve these precious items because of the tremendous destruction of the art in Tibet itself since the Chinese occupation. Since the Dalai Lama and 100,000 followers left Tibet in 1959, there has been widespread buying and selling of Tibetan art due to economic necessity and the changed way of life. Interestingly, traditional Tibetans still consider commercial dealings in religious art immoral and disrespectful, since this trade shows a lack of appreciation for the ritual purposes for which the art was created.

Notes

1. Loden Sherap Dagyab, *Tibetan Religious Art*, Part I (Weisbaden: Otto Harrassowitz, 1977), pp.20-23.

2. Rechung Rinpoche, Jampal Kunzang, *A Short Study of the Origin and Evolution of Different Styles of Buddhist Paintings and Iconography* (Sikkim: Institute of Tibetology, n.d.).

3. Dagyab Rinpoche, op.cit., p.22.

4. Alice Getty, *The Gods of Northern Buddhism* (Oxford: Clarendon Press, 1928), p.17.

5. According to rumor, the Chinese removed the statue from the temple and sold it to a Tibetan Mongolian monastery in Russia. It is now said to be preserved in a museum in Ulan-Ude, north of Mongolia near Lake Baikal, Russia.

6. Dagyab Rinpoche, op.cit., p.22.

13 *The Thangka according to Tradition*

José Ignacio Cabezón and
Geshe Thubten Tendar
Sera Je Monastic University
Bylakuppe, India

[Based in part on an oral interview with Gelong Lobsang Tenzing and Gelong Lobzang Dondrup, artists in residence at the Sera Monastic University, and on a short unpublished text of Gonsar Rinpoche.]

The *rGyal rab sba bzhed*, a Tibetan historical chronicle, states that the art of Buddhist Tibet began in the eighth century during the reign of King Khri srong lde'u btsan. During the construction of the first Buddhist monastery, *bSam yas* (Samye), the artist *rGya mtshan ma can*—considered to be the human incarnation of a divine being—asked the Indian monk-scholar Śāntarakṣita, one of the major figures in the spread of Buddhism to Tibet, whether he ought to follow the Indian or Chinese style in the representation of deities. Śāntarakṣita answered that, since the Buddha had been born in India, he should follow this tradition. The king, however, felt that it was not sufficient to adopt a completely foreign style. Since his aim was to arouse the faith of his people, he felt that the deities ought to be represented in a way that was compatible with Tibetan aesthetics. With this end in mind, the representation of the deity Avalokitesvara (*sPyan ras gzigs*) was modeled after *Khu sTag tshab*, considered the most beautiful man; the goddess Tara (*sGrol ma*) was modeled after *lCog ro gZa' lha bu sman*, the most beautiful woman, and so forth. This was the origin of Buddhist art in Tibet according to traditional sources.

Since then many different schools of thangka (religious scroll) painting have flourished. Three are considered the most important: the *sMan ri*, *mKhyen ri* and *Kar bris*. From among these, the *sMan ri* is considered most influential. *sMan ri* was founded by the noted fifteenth century artist and scholar, *sMan thang pa*, whose texts are considered fundamental works in all the various schools. Apparently, the other minor schools evolved from the above three.

The technique of thangka painting begins with a fine linen cloth called *ka shi*, the ancient name for Benares, the city in India that is considered the source of the best linen. The cloth is first stretched over a frame. Several coats of a type of gesso called *ka rag*, a chalk-like substance mixed with glue, are applied to the surface of the cloth and made smooth. The next step consists of tracing the outlines of figures to be included according to the proper grids that assure the correct proportions of the figures' bodies. The Buddha figures, those of other masters, and peaceful deities are based on the grid of the Buddha Sakyamuni. The grid is the most important one and the first to be taught to the novice. The figure of peaceful female deities is based on the grid of the goddess Tara, while the form of wrathful deities is based on the grid of the deity Vajrapāni.

After tracing the outline, the artist proceeds with the initial application of color. There are four principal colors used: blue, yellow, white, and red. In Tibet these were obtained by grinding special stones the brilliance of which was said never to attenuate but only to increase with time. All colors used by thangka painters can be obtained by properly mixing these four basic colors in the correct proportions. Shading, considered one of the most difficult procedures, is the next step. In addition, it was common practice to paint the bodies of deities with gold as an offering to them. Tibet had an abundant supply of gold, but the best quali-

Drawing the Deity on the Thangka Cloth, Lhasa. Photo: Philip Sugden

Painting the Background of the Thangka, Lhasa. Photo: Philip Sugden

ty gold dust used in painting was prepared by the Nepali craftsmen who lived in Lhasa.

The final step for completing the thangka is called *spyan 'byed* or "the opening of the eyes." This stage consists of painting the eyes of the deity while certain prayers are recited. Finally, the syllables *oṁ*, *āh*, and *hūṁ* (the symbols of body, speech, and mind) are written on the back of the painting at the spots corresponding to the crown, throat, and heart of each figure. Again, as an offering, the painting is framed in silk brocade of different colors, usually imported from Russia, China, Mongolia, or even from Japan.

Definite spiritual practices accompany the art of thangka painting. The ideal painter is said to be a fully ordained monk (*dge slong*). He should also be an initiate of the Tantras. To the extent that the painting is to be used as an aid in visualizing one's self as the deity (the essence of Tantric practice), it is incumbent upon artists to visualize themselves as the deity and all of their implements as being of the same nature as the divinity while the painting is being executed. Moreover, the four principal colors, together with the color green, are to be visualized as being of the same nature as the five Buddhas (*rGyal ba rigs nga*). This, of course, is the ideal. Not every painter, however, has either the ability or the will to engage in these practices.

On the more mundane side, artists usually work on commissions, the majority of which came from individuals. However, the situation in Lhasa was an exception to this rule. In the capital city, the Guild of Thangka Painters was not only the source of all artwork commissions by the government, but was also a learning center where young artists could apprentice themselves to the more experienced masters in order to learn the craft. The three highest offices within the guild were (in descending order or rank) the *dbu drung*, *dbu chen*, and *dbu chung*. In 1959 before the final Chinese occupation, the rank of *dbu drung*, the most prestigious, was held by only three individuals, two laymen and one monk. The number of guild members was said to have varied from fifty to several hundred. The guild itself was divided into two sections: one was concerned mostly with thangka and mural painting and the other with wooden figurines and wood painting. The two sections did not always coexist peacefully with each other; at one point, they separated for a period of several months. The guild, however, was non-sectarian, ad-

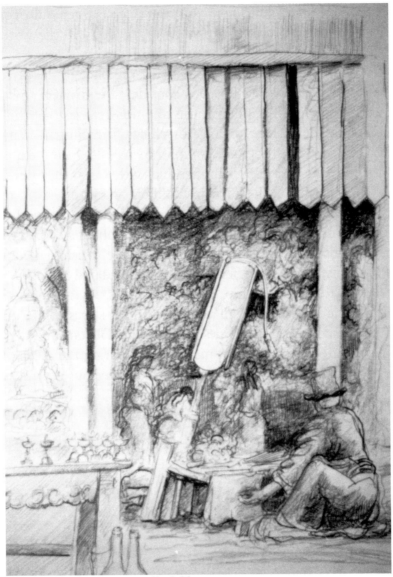

Altar at Hemis Monastery, Ladakh.   Graphite Drawing—John Westmore

mitting members from all of the major sects of Tibetan Buddhism.

When a work of religious art is finished, it is generally brought to a *bla ma* for consecration (*rab gnas*). During this ritual, which is often quite complex, the wisdom being (*ye shes pa*) that corresponds to the deity in the work is invited to enter the work in order to become one with it (*gnyis su med pa*). From this point on, the figure is said to contain the living presence of the divinity. Being in the presence of a consecrated image is considered equivalent to being before the enlightened being itself. Although the tradition realizes that this awareness may be impossible for ordinary beings to achieve, it maintains that those who have attained the level of spiritual accomplishment called the ''Samādhi of the Stream of the Doctrine'' can see paintings and statues as if they were the deities themselves. That is why, in the Tibetan tradition, works of art are treated with veneration, and why they are placed on altars and worshiped with offerings.

On the other hand, the tradition makes clear that enlightened beings have gone beyond the need for offerings. Hence, it is the disciple's wish to accumulate merit and not the deity's need for offerings that is considered to be the motivation behind the act of religious worship. In the process of paying homage to the enlightened ones, the adept is said to accumulate great stores of merit that in the future will ripen into spiritual qualities. This is why Tibetan Buddhists consider any religious work of art a ''field of merit.'' By planting the seeds of virtue on this fertile soil, the disciple is said to gain the most precious of fruits: the attainment of buddhahood.

14　The Flowering of Tibetan Architecture

Stephen White

Introduction

Tibetan architecture is really a Himalayan cultural expression, extending beyond the boundaries of what has been known as Tibet to other areas of the Himalaya where Mahayana Buddhism, the Greater Vehicle, is practiced. From west to east this cultural region includes Ladakh, Lahoul and Spiti (now in India); Nepal; Tibet; Sikkim (also in India) and Bhutan. The continuity of Tibetan architecture and culture into the modern world where a developed traditional expression has survived intact is a rare occurrence. The poignancy of this continuity is that it exerts itself, and is still developing, in the face of the twentieth century's rising expectations and political rearrangements.

Earlier, when borders were open for the people of the Himalaya, a freer, sustaining exchange of culture and form was possible. With the absorption of Tibet into China in the 1950s, this has changed. Tibetan culture and its expression in architecture are now confronted by the challenge of maintaining identities without connection back to Tibet itself, where Tibetan culture no longer flourishes. Tibetan architecture, though, continues to flower in the Himalaya, as it has for hundreds of years. The act of building is a vehicle for continuing the tenets of Buddhism and is an expression of the undaunted Tibetan identity. A most remarkable new development is the appearance of Tibetan architecture in communities throughout India where thousands of Tibetans fled following the Dalai Lama in 1959—a new inspiring breath of life and hope for Tibetan culture in the land where Buddhism began.

Tibetan Architecture: Characteristics, Variations, Meanings

The forms of Tibetan architecture spring from a combination of Buddhist philosophy and responses to natural conditions in the places that make up the built world of the Himalaya—forts, palaces, temples, monasteries, and houses as the occupied buildings, with stupa and chorten monuments and the Buddhist way around and in between. Place and building play a major role in establishing a sense of Buddhist identity—providing settings for ceremonies, incorporating symbols of past events or cosmic diagrams into form, and offering a continuing fabric of meaningful places.

Elements of Architecture

Tibetan buildings are charactrized by their massive walls, interior wooden column and beam structures, lighter often intricately carved and painted wood windows and doors, and flat roofs. The walls, built on rubble foundations, are made either of stone, mud brick, or an earth and gravel mixture, depending on which materials are locally available.[1] Mud brick walls are common for buildings in Ladakh, and mud or cut stone is common in parts of Tibet. In Bhutan and Eastern Tibet a rammed earth technique where loose earth is put into forms and compressed with wooden mallets is common. Each method gives a particular quality to the buildings in the different areas, within a structural logic common to all: plain walls heavier at the bottom, tapering gently as they rise upward, with more and larger openings for windows near the top.

Within the enclosure of the walls is a timber column and beam structure, supporting both upper floors and the roof. The Tibetan word for column is *khar,*

Potala Palace, Lhasa, Tibet.   Photo: Philip Sugden

for beam *dhuma*. These elements provide a module which is used to describe the size of a room—a two-*khar*, three-*khar* room, etc.—and take on a symbolic aspect for certain rooms. Scripture halls, *tsug-lug-khang*, are generally of four *khar* and eight *dhuma*, representing the Four Noble Truths and the Eightfold Path.[2] Columns and beams can be quite elaborately carved and painted. They have additional symbolism, including representations of the lotus "...the image of purity and enlightenment which symbolizes the Boddhisattva's attitude..;"[3] *chos brtsegs*,"[4] meaning "stacked up," a kind of stepping form which symbolizes the scritures of the lamas piled one on top of the other; or sometimes Ganesh, the elephant God, representing "...the bringing of peace, of conquering and overcoming interferences."[5]

Windows and doors are correspondingly carved and painted where appropriate to the use and ceremony of the building. Windows also often have a short white curtain called a *shimbu* around the top, to protect paintings there from sunshine, with symbolic meaning derived from the auspicious color white, here representing "...an open net of jewels."[6] The curtains are removed and changed in relation to several occasions—the arrival of a new year, or the enthronement or death of a Dalai Lama.

Roofs are generally flat and constructed of joists that span the beams. The joists carry smaller perpendicular wood members covered with small stones and earth. A final layer of "archa" stones, very hard but light, is added on top. After being sprinkled with water and then pounded down, which fuses them together, the "archa" forms a continuous waterproof layer. The making of Tibetan buildings is a communal activity, with many people from the village or town coming to help with construction. This final act of enclosing the building and pounding the "archa" is accompanied by singing, stories, and laughter.[7]

Particular variations above the roof line distinguish the architecture of different regions of the Himalaya, or signify a building's importance. An entablature of twigs used for fuel is stacked at the roof edge, a characteristic of many of the buildings of Ladakh and Tibet. Where there is more rainfall in Nepal and Bhutan, a sloping wooden roof is added. In Bhutan this roofed area is quite large and used for storage and living space.[8] On some buildings in Tibet, such as Tashilhunpo Monastery, magnificent curving golden roofs are built above important ceremonial rooms. On temples, the four corners are often marked by "victory banners," commemorating the victory of Sakye Pandita over Trokye Gawa in a long past debate of philosophy.[9]

Stupa and Chorten

Built of earth and stone at sites considered to be sacred, the *stupa* originated in India in the third century B.C.E. as a hemispherical Buddhist reliquary and as a place for burial. It is a complex expression, composed of the cosmic diagram of the mandala—superimposed circles and squares in a plan within which is found the image of the deity—with a column at its center embedded in the solid mound which is the focus of worship. The column is variously thought of as the vertical cosmic axis[10] and as a representation of the tree of life.[11] The elements of the stupa ". . . should be regarded as visual aids for the contemplation of the formless truth that is beyond them all."[12]

Pilgrimage to stupas is a ritual of great importance, with the clockwise circum-

Farm House, Jiazhiaghou, Amdo, Tibet.   Photo: Carole Elchert

ambulation of the stupa a purification of the pilgrim's "negativities and misdeeds."[13] The present Dalai Lama has written that the basis for pilgrimage is also "...to draw some positive force from a blessed place, so that one's own merit, the store of good qualities within one's mind, will increase."[14] Major stupas are at Sanchi in India, and at Bodhnath and Swayambhunath in Nepal.

The stupa was transformed in terms of size, symbolism and name into the Tibetan *chorten* as it made its way into the Himalaya after Padmasambhava brought Buddhism to Tibet in 645 C.E. In Tibet there is a great stupa at Shigatse, but more common is the smaller chorten, literally "a receptacle for offerings." The mound of the stupa is reduced and set on top of a pedestal in the chorten, and can take on eight variations in form, each associated with a different quality such as divine manifestation, emanation of happiness, victory, nirvana.[15] Chortens are built to hold important texts and objects. They are also built as a shrine for a deceased lama, and as a means to establish territory or to counteract other forces present. There is a story of a chorten built at the northern border region of Tibet to encounter intrusion by the Mongolians. Songtsen Gampo, a great master of central Tibet, knew intuitively that the "chorten was falling down, and sent volunteers to go rebuild it and re-establish the reliquary. Later, when the chorten was finished, he blessed it from far away.[16]

Choosing a Site and The Act of Building

Choosing a building site is based on varying concerns, from practical ones such as security, orientation, and relation to farmland to more symbolic ones for a temple which is built where "...a plot of land possessing good characteristics is the foundation from which all happiness is produced."[17] In the city of Leh in Ladakh, buildings are grouped close together on land that cannot be easily irrigated. An overlooking palace, temples and fortresses higher up the protecting slope all face south to the sun. A few small farmhouses are set among the terraced fields of barley beyond. Lhasa and the Potala Palace in Tibet follow something of a similar pattern. By contrast, in Bhutan there is a concentration of fort, monastery, temple, government center into the Bhutanese *dzong* at each valley center, with farmhouses sprinkled throughout the valley beyond.

Choosing a site for a temple is a demanding and precise undertaking, done after evaluating auspicious signs about orientation, location of rivers, roads, soil, and landforms. From among a great array of influences, a site for a temple is sought that has the following attributes:

> ...a tall mountain behind and many hills in front, two rivers converging in front from the right and left, a central valley of rocks and meadows resembling heaps of grain, and a lower part which is like two hands crossed at the wrists."[18]

Chapels are found at the innermost spaces of the temple. These rooms, containing images and statues of the Buddha, are considered the residences of the deity.[19] When not part of discrete temples which take their place in the landscape, chapels form a part of monastic complexes, which include cells for monks,

Potala Palace, Lhasa.

Photograph—Carole Elchert

Drigung Monastery.

Pastel Drawing—John Westmore

Nomad Family, Chang Tang Plateau, Tibet.　　　　　Photograph—Carole Elchert

Tingri, Tibet.　　　　　Photograph—Carole Elchert

Rongbuck Monastery, Tibet.   Pastel Drawing—John Westmore

Yamdrok Valley from Samding Monastery.   Pastel Drawing—John Westmore

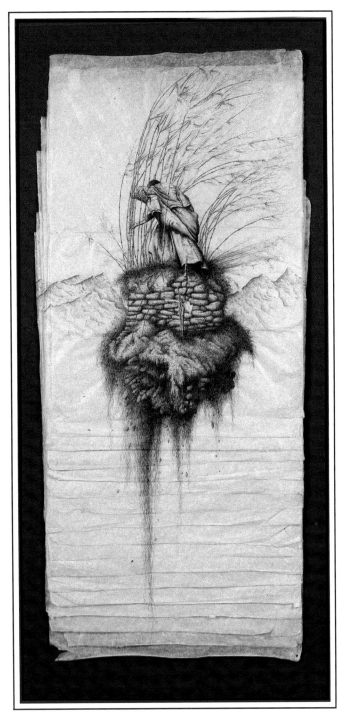

Tribute to the Ethers.
Ink on Handmade Himalayan Papers—Philip Sugden

Nomad Girl, Tibet.
Photograph—Carole Elchert

Sisters at Shekar, Tibet.
Photograph—Carole Elchert

Nomad Father and Son, Tibet.
Photograph—Philip Sugden

Tibetan in his Barley Mill, Labrang, Tibet.

Photograph—Carole Elchert

Rainbow over Shechen Tennyi Dargyeling Monastery, Bodha, Nepal.   Photograph—Roger Sugden

Illumination at Swayambhu, Nepal.   Photograph—Roger Sugden

Exile and Other States of Nirvana #2.

Ink and Gouache on Paper—Philip Sugden

The Final Frontier.   Ink and Gouache on Paper—Philip Sugden

Chang Tang Plateau, Tibet.

Pastel Drawing—John Westmore

Mani Stone and the Lhotse Massif.

Photograph—Roger Sugden

Norbulinka, Ladakh.

Photograph—Carole Elchert

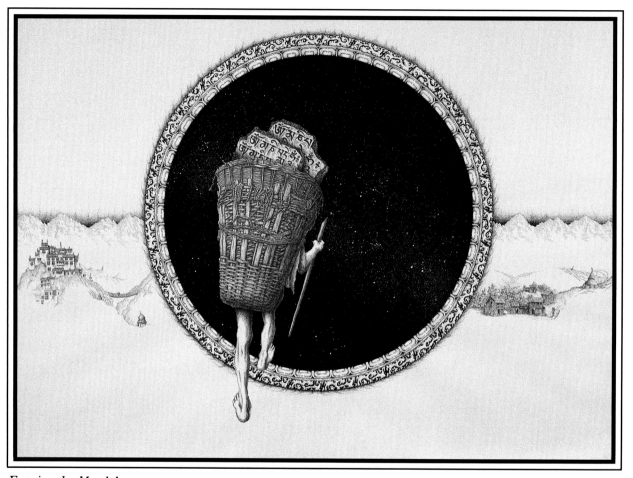

Entering the Mandala.

Ink and Gouache on Paper—Philip Sugden

East Meets West, Lamayuru Monastery, Ladakh.   Photograph—Carole Elchert

Prayer Flag Series #3.

Ink on Handmade Paper—Philip Sugden

Tibetan Landscape.

Pastel Drawing—John Westmore

Prayer Flag Series, Fragments from Another World. Ink on Handmade Himalayan Paper—Philip Sugden

Tibetan Woman of Amdo , Tibet.

Photograph—Carole Elchert

Milarepa's Cave Temple, Nyalam, Tibet.

Pastel Drawing—John Westmore

Chorten at Gyantse, Tibet. Photograph—Carole Elchert

Kumbum Monastery, Eastern Tibet. Photograph—Carole Elchert

Father and Son, Nomads near Rorgai, Tibet.
Photograph—Carole Elchert

Nomad Girl on Horseback, Rorgai, Tibet.
Photograph—Carole Elchert

Young Monks with Photo of His Holiness the Dalai Lama.
Photograph—Carole Elchert

Study for Exile and Other States of Nirvana.   Graphite on Paper—Philip Sugden

Monk with Prayer Book at Tsurphu Monastery, Tibet. Photograph—Carole Elchert

Chortens at Shey Monastery, Ladakh.   Photo: Philip Sugden

storage, a kitchen, and often a large south-facing courtyard which functions as a meeting place where all may assemble.

The importance of choosing a site and building with care cannot be underestimated. The entire process reveals the making of architecture as a vehicle assisting enlightenment. A sacred sutra explains it this way:

> ...the virtue of correctly erecting a temple and installing in it shrines, and offering a dwelling, bed and refreshment to the monastic assembly, increases ever more and more, and will not become exhausted even in a thousand million aeons.[20]

The Flowering of Tibetan Architecture in India

Tibet is a remote country on the high plains beyond the Himalaya. There is little doubt that its geographic isolation contributed to the continuity of Tibet's traditional culture and architecture over centuries. In the nineteenth and early twentieth centuries, though, Tibet had to close its borders in an attempt to maintain its integrity as the forces of the British and Russian empires and China extended themselves across Asia. In the end this plan was without success. In 1959 the fourteenth Dalai Lama, Tibet's spiritual and political leader, fled from the Chinese to India followed by thousands of Tibetans. Many others scattered across the world. In the aftermath, the main institutions of Tibetan culture in Tibet—monasteries, temples and shrines—were destroyed by the Communist Chinese who attempted to eradicate Buddhism and Tibetan identity. As the face of Tibet was eroded, the Dalai Lama appealed to exiled Tibetans to remember the value of their own culture while they adapted themselves to their new surroundings.

As a consequence of the displacement from the "Land of Snows," however, a new expression of Tibetan culture is rising in India, accompanied by a new flowering of Tibetan architecture as Tibetans re-establish their institutions and build shelter for themselves in new communities. The freshness, excitement and belief in the virtue of continuing their culture is evident in the new architecture. At a fundamental level, Tibetans would be refugees without these buildings, in surroundings unlike those they had known.

Jigme Taring and the Memory of Tibetan Architecture

The continuing vitality of Tibetan architecture in India is in great measure due to the memory and energy of Jigme Taring, who fled to India with the Dalai Lama in 1959. Mr. Taring was Prince of Sikkim, cabinet minister, and architect of the Tibetan government in Lhasa. He is credited with creating many buildings in Tibet, including the Dalai Lama's summer palace at Norbu Linka,[21] completed in 1949. On arrival in India after crossing the Himalaya, he was asked by the Dalai Lama to draw a plan of Lhasa showing its important places. The Dalai Lama feared that sacred and historic buildings might not survive the Chinese invasion. From memory, Taring re-created the city of Lhasa on one map, and the surrounding valley and its monasteries on another. Three of the monasteries—Sera, Ganden, and Drepung—were forceably abandoned and since have been largely destroyed. In 1976, Taring achieved a long-standing ambition

Tsug-lug-khang (Jokhang) Temple, Lhasa.   Photo: Carole Elchert

to draw floor plans from memory of Tibet's most important building, the main Buddhist scripture hall in Lhasa, the *Tsug-lug-khang,* and its main inner temple, the Jokhang, begun in the seventh century and still standing. Taring wrote in 1976:

> The sad news of the destruction of many thousands of monasteries by the Communist Chinese has given added impetus to me to realize my ambition. My main purpose is to enable our younger generation to have at least an idea of the historical building from both the cultural and religious point of view. I worked for eighteen years in the Tsu-lug-khang....as such I can clearly visualize the whole structure of this famous center of devotion and most of the statues in each and every chapel.[22]

In 1981, Taring and his grandson Tenzin Norbu (who had recently arrived in India from Tibet without knowledge of his grandparents after years of separation) became acquainted while they built a scale model of the *Tsug-lug-khang.*

The model now tours Tibetan settlements in India, thus continuing the memory of Tibet's most important building. The Tarings' garden at their home in north India recalls the garden they left behind in Lhasa. Each has a similar circular plan with an evergreen at the center.

Mr. Taring served as Principal of the Central Tibetan School in Mussoorie from 1960 to 1975. There he designed the first new Tibetan buildings to be built in India, a chorten and a temple. With Romi Khosla of India, he also designed the Library of Tibetan Works and Archives in Dharamsala which was completed in 1971.

Tibetan Settlements in India

Since 1949, many settlements have been built by Tibetans in India's Himalayan foothills, and several were built in south India on gifts of land from the Indian government. In these Tibetan enclaves, forms and meanings of ancient Tibetan architecture are being re-established in a wholly different culture and climate. India is a country of great numbers struggling to modernize; of Hindu and Muslim faith; of heat, rain, and dust. From difficult, disorienting beginnings—the abandoned British hill station, Dharamsala, in north India where the Dalai Lama began his appeal for cultural preservation, to south India where Tibetans living in tents surrounded by jungle worshipped before one makeshift altar and the precious Buddha image given by His Holiness[23]—Tibetan places have taken hold, grown and spread. Tibetan architecture exerts itself anew as a Himalayan expression in India, built by a collaboration of Tibetans, Hindu laborers, Bhutanese, and Sikkimese sculptors and artists.

The new buildings in India are mostly temples, monasteries, and chortens, constructed of concrete but with forms and artwork similar to those present in the older buildings of stone, mud, and wood. At Bir, near Dharamsala in Himachal Pradesh, four new monasteries have been built. The familiar pattern of courtyard and temple surrounded by monks' rooms is continued here. The first monastery one arrives at is called, "Phelyul Choekhorling," meaning "glorious country, religious hill, island" was designed by its head lama, Venerable Rigo Tulku Rinpoche, to re-institute the monastery with the same name as the one he left be-

Labrang Monastery, Amdo, Tibet. Photo: Carole Elchert

hind in Tibet. Since they are new, the buildings, paintings, and sculptures are crisp and bright—a fresh expression of Tibetan culture. Images of the four guardians of the faith—Dhitarashtra, Virudhaka, Viruphaksha, and Kuvera[24]—protect the entrance to the temple. On the upper level, sculptures by Bhutanese artists are currently underway. When completed, they will form a three-dimensional representation of an older thangka painting. At nearby Tashi Jong monastery, completed in 1976, the courtyard is the scene for the traditional lama dance which takes place under a ceremonial Tibetan tent erected for the occasion and decorated with one of the eight auspicious signs. On the outskirts of India's capital, New Delhi, a new Buddhist study centre painted by Sikkimese artists is rising in sight of the Qutab Minar, the enormous masonry column built from the destruction of Hindu shrines which established the first Muslim presence in India almost eight hundred years ago.

Dharamsala has become the Tibetan's capital-in-exile, and is often called "Little Lhasa in India." There the Nechung Monastery, home of the state oracle of Tibet and the Namgyal Monastery, the Dalai Lama's personal monastery, have been re-instituted. Nechung in Dharamsala, designed to resemble the Nechung buildings in Tibet, is a smaller version reflective of its diminished population of monks. Under the cover of tall trees, new houses cascade down the hillsides in typical Tibetan fashion. The *Lingkhor*, or "Holy Walk," with prayer stones and flags along the path for circumambulating the Dalai Lama's residence, has also been re-created in Dharamsala.[25]

A remarkable new building in Dharamsala is the Tsug-lug-khang, said to be designed by the Dalai Lama himself.[26] Built on a promontory across from the Dalai Lama's residence, it contains the same spatial patterns as traditional buildings, but with an openness, spareness and lack of decoration more typical of modern construction. The Dalai Lama has said that the events of the past century perhaps signify a need for Tibetans to purify themselves. This building presents the fundamental principles of Buddhist space distilled to their essences: the selection of an appropriate site, a circumambulation route around the temple and objects of worship (in this case of one of them being the Dalai Lama himself as he sits inside), figures of the Buddha, and the lama's seat at its center. Rooms for His Holiness, a private chapel, and attendants' rooms are on the upper level. The extended porch at the front of the building is the scene of frequent debates by monks from the adjacent Namgyal Monastery. Their questions can be heard many times during the day and evening. The clap by one monk signaling a question to be answered, and the subsequent reply by another monk echo out across the open air of Dharamsala. Tibetan culture is alive and passing on to another generation, and the new Tibetan architecture in India is providing a meaningful setting for its continuation.

The Lotus

The lotus appears frequently in Tibetan Buddhist art: in painting, sculpture, and architecture as a symbol of enlightenment and the purity of the enlightened mind. One of its lesser known aspects is that the lotus blooms from the mire. To the tragedy of the uprooting of Tibetan culture, this may offer some sign of hope. For out of the mire of suffering and loss, a vigorous bloom of new Tibetan architecture has opened in India to support Tibetan life there. This complements the already continuing Buddhist cultures and architectures of the Himalaya that have thus far been outside the path of destruction.

It is clear that the creation of Tibetan enclaves in other lands can never be a substitute for the harmony and scope of life in what was a more seamless, enduring Buddhist landscape. But the creation of Tibetan architecture in India has offered the chance for Tibetans to live in relative peace, with some sense of identity in their "home away from home" as Rinchen Dolma Taring (the first General Secretary of the Tibetan Homes Fundation for orphans in India and wife of Jigme Taring) has written in her autobiography.[27]

It may be beneficial for all to ponder some of the issues raised by the example of the continued life of the Tibetans—the potential for art and architecture to root us, however temporarily, in the world; the persistence of life and the human spirit; the chance for renewal—and to remember how tenuously held that life is.

Greatest thanks for assistance in preparation of this article goes to Jigme Taring and his grandson, Tenzin Norbu, for their introduction to Tibetan architecture, its history and construction practices; and to several people at the Library of Tibetan Works and Archives (LTWA) in Dharamsala, India. Gyatsho Tshering, Director, coordinated the efforts extended by the LTWA, and Thupten Sangye, Research Officer, gave generously of his time in several interviews. Thupten Tashi, Research Assistant, made arrangements for trips to the newly founded Tibetan monasteries in Himachal Pradesh, and gave valuable translations and interpretations at these sites. Marion Kramm White assisted with research.

Footnotes

1. Jigme Taring, former architect of the Tibetan government in Lhasa, now residing in India; interview with the author; Rajpur, India; November 1988.

2. Tenzin Norbu, Tibetan painter and carpenter, who arrived in India from Tibet in 1981; interview with the author; New Delhi, India; November 1988.

3. Thupten Sangye, Research Officer, Library of Tibetan Works and Archives; interview with the author; Dharamsala, India; November 1988.

4. Thubten Legshay Gyatsho, *Gateway to the Temple*, p. 30.

5. Thupten Sangye, op. cit.

6. Idem.

7. Jigme Taring, op. cit.

8. Corneille Jest and Joseph Allen Stein, ''Architecture in Bhutan and Ladakh,'' *The Himalaya: Aspects of Change*, p. 299.

9. Thupten Tashi, Research Assistant, Library of Tibetan Works and Archives; interview with the author; Dharamsala, India; November 1988.

10. Valerio Sestini and Enzo Somigli, *Sherpa Architecture*, p. 32.

11. Romi Khosla, *Buddhist Monasteries of the Western Himalaya*, p. 85.

12. Nelson Wu, *Chinese and Indian Architecture*, p. 14.

13. Tenzin Gyatso, 14th Dalai Lama of Tibet, as quoted in Avedon, *In Exile From The Land of Snows*, p. 208.

14. Thupten Sangye, op. cit.

15. Khosla, op. cit., p. 85.

16. Thupten Sangye, op. cit.

17. Thubten Legshay Gyatsho, op. cit., p. 30.

18. Ibid., p. 29.

19. Khosla, op. cit., p. 82.

20. Saddharmasmrtyupasthana Sutra, as quoted in Thubten Legshay Gyatsho, *Gateway to the Temple*, p. 33.

21. Gyatsho Tshering, Director, Library of Tibetan Works and Archives; correspondence with the author, October 1988.

22. Jigme Taring, *The Index and Plan of Lhasa Cathedral*, p. 1.

23. John Avedon, *In Exile From The Land of Snows*, pp. 108-114.

24. Khosla, op. cit., p. 82.

25. Avedon, op. cit., p. 133.

26. Gyatsho Tshering, Director, Library of Tibetan Works and Archives; interview with the author; Dharamsala, India, November 1988.

27. Rinchen Dolma Taring, *Daughter of Tibet*, p. 315.

Bibliography

Aris, Michael. *Views of Medieval Bhutan: The Diary and Drawings of Samuel Davis.* New Delhi: Roli Books, 1982.

Avedon, John F. *In Exile From The Land Of Snows.* London: Wisdom Tibet, 1985.

Jest, Corneille and Joseph Allen Stein. "Architecture in Bhutan and Ladakh," *The Himalaya: Aspects of Change.* Delhi: India International Centre and Oxford University Press, 1981.

Khosla, Romi. *Buddhist Monasteries in the Western Himalaya.* Kathmandu: Ratna Pustak Bhandar, 1979.

Rowell, Galen. *Mountains of the Middle Kingdom.* San Francisco: Sierra Club, 1983.

Sestini, Valerio and Enzo Somigli. *Sherpa Architecture.* Translated by Timothy Paterson. Paris: UNESCO, 1978.

Taring, Jigme. *The Index and Plan of Lhasa Cathedral in Tibet.* Rajpur: Jigme Taring, 1976.

Taring, Jigme. *Map of Lhasa.* Drawn by Zasak J. Taring, edited by Chie Nakane. Tokyo: University of Tokyo Press, 1984.

Taring, Rinchen Dolma. *Daughter of Tibet: The Autobiography of Rinchen Dolma Taring.* London: Wisdom Tibet, 1986.

Thubten Legshay Gyatsho. *Gateway To The Temple*. Kathmandu: Ratna Pustak Bhandar, 1979.

Wu, Nelson I. *Chinese and Indian Architecture*. New York, Braziller, 1963.

Drigung Monastery.

Pastel Drawing—John Westmore

15 *Tibetan Language*

José Ignacio Cabezón

Tibetan language, like its people, culture, and its religious traditions, is unique. Linguistically classified in the Tibeto-Burman language group, Tibetan more closely resembles the language of its southern neighbor, Burma (and other related languages such as K'iang, Moso, and Jyarung), than the other languages of Asia. Indeed, the Tibetans and Burmese still share many words in common.

Although the Tibetan language is probably quite old as a spoken tongue, the written language, according to traditional accounts, dates from about the seventh century C.E. (common era). Unlike Chinese, which is a pictographic language, Tibetan utilizes an alphabet. Some scholars have speculated that before the present script was acquired in the seventh century, another form of Tibetan writing existed. Several historical works refer to a letter written by King *Srong btsan sgam po* (Songtsen Gampo) to the king of Nepal.

This letter would have been written before the acquisition of the present script from India. These discoveries led scholars to surmise the existence of an earlier written form, related in some way to the language of Bon, the native religion of Tibet.

The earliest example of Tibetan script still preserved is the Zhol stone pillar inscription which dates to the middle of the eighth century. Dated several centuries later, the earliest preserved texts are those found in the caves at Tun huang. They are interesting linguistically because of the variations in spelling. These texts suggest that even at this time the language was quite flexible and not yet standardized.

Two main scripts are popular among the Tibetans today: the *dbu can*, or printed form, and *dbu med*, or cursive form, which can be subdivided into the *ka ring*, *tshugs*, *tshugs ma khyug*, and *khyug*. A related script called *phags pa*, named after the *Sa skya bla ma* (Sakya lama) by the same name (d. 1280), is said to have been invented by Phags pa (Phagpa) as a writing system for the Mongolian language. It is not, however, a functioning script in Tibet. The *dbu can* form is the principal medium for literary works while government documents and epistolary tracts are more common in the *dbu med*.

Made obvious in this chapter, Tibetan words contain many compounded consonant clusters that are unpronounced. This makes the pronunciation of Tibetan words a daunting task for the uninitiated. The word for an incarnate *bla ma* (lama), *sprul sku* is roughly pronounced in modern Lhasa dialect "tool-koo." Whether this was always the case or whether many of these prefixes and suffixes were originally pronounced is not known. Nevertheless, in Tibetan border areas such as Ladakh, many of the consonants that are omitted in the dialect of central Tibet are pronounced. This has led some scholars to speculate that in the early period Tibetan was pronounced in a way that generally resembled the written form.

Though the alphabet and standardization of the language served definite political ends, the chief motivating factors for the creation of a Tibetan alphabet were religious. In order for the classical texts of Indian Buddhism to be translated into Tibetan, a literary medium needed to exist. With this end in mind, the Tibetan king *Srong btsan sgam po* (d.650 C.E.) is said to have sent a delegation of Tibetans under the leadership of Thon mi sambhota to India. As a result of his study of the India writing system, Thon mi developed a Tibetan script modeled after the Indian Gupta alphabet that had been in use in North India since the fourth century C.E. Thon mi is also credited with composing the first Tibetan grammars: the *Sum cu pa* and *rTags kyi 'jug pa*. After the invention of the script, the translation of the Sanskrit texts into Tibetan began and with it, the spread of

Pilgrims at Karma Dupgyu Monastery, Ladakh.   Photo: Philip Sugden

Pilgrims at the Jokhang Temple, Lhasa.   Watercolor—John Westmore

Mani Stones.   Ink Drawing—Philip Sugden

Buddhism into the country.

   The classical written Tibetan language, the medium for the translation of San-skrit texts and for the composition of indigenous religious literature, differs sub-stantially from the spoken vernacular. Though a great deal of oral material exists in the form of folk tales, these oral works have not been put into written form until very recently. Hence the oral and literary tradition have developed indepen-dently from the earliest time. In their literature, the epistolary style, which is quite ancient, and the more modern journalistic style of writing are intermediary forms between the colloquial and the classical language. As for oral works, the same can be said of the format of spoken religious discourse which, though oral, borrows a great deal (lexically and syntactically) from the classical language.

   Although the dialects associated with different geographical areas, such as Kham, Amdo, U and Tsang, vary considerably, most modern day Tibetans can under-stand each other with little difficulty. The fact that all of these geographical regions share the same script, despite variations in pronunciation, gives a uniformity to the language that is missing in any other South Asian contexts.

16 *Tibetan Literature*

David Templeman

Early writers on Tibet often dismissed the literature of the "Land of the Snows" as exclusively limited to lengthy Buddhist texts laboriously translated from Sanskrit into Tibetan, and equally long "native" commentaries on such works. Apart from the passing reference to the extraordinary number of prayer texts, and the odd writings which even the briefest of residencies among Tibetans could not fail to bring to one's attention (*The Book of the Dead* and *The Life of Milarepa*), these early writers were quite perfunctory in passing off Tibetan literature as stylized, lengthy, and static.

Due to the efforts of translators, scholars, linguists, and others, a vast treasury of writings has been revealed, showing a breadth of subject matter not previously suspected. The nature of the West has dictated the need for Buddhist material to be the first fruits of translation, but even here much is distinctively Tibetan.

From its earliest origins in a folk literature of professions of fealty to one's ruler, songs of challenge, and annals of tribal affairs, the Tibetan style was mostly couched in images which reflect the wild and untamed nature of the land itself. To an extent, many features of this early style remain in current folk literature. The same images delight and evoke the same responses in modern Tibetans as they did long ago. Allusions to wild geographical features, such as hair-raising precipices, plains of battle, and cloud-wreathed peaks, are tempered with accurate and curiously tender observations of Tibet's natural, untouched world of alpine flowers and abundant wildlife. R. A. Stein's pages on the literature of Tibet show this beautiful mixture quite clearly in expressions which speak of the lone tiger in the southern bamboo forests, the soaring vulture with its white belly flashing, and the mighty wild yak killed by an arrow fashioned from southern bamboo and fletched with eagle feathers.[1] These images stir a strong sense of a possible time when such creatures and forests formed an intimate part of daily life, especially in the readers who have seen the remnants of the mighty forests and the depleted wildlife on the Tibetan plateau.

Tibetans also traditionally delight in wit-sharpening riddling, often extemporized. In the sixth to eighth centuries C.E., riddling formed part of a courtly ritual by the sacrificers to the Emperor in tent courts of Tibetan warrior-rulers. Even today, the impulse to create riddles is strong. Some of my own fondest memories are of walking among hills and forests improvising riddles and laughing, echo upon echo, with my companions. Riddles important to folk literature include these: ''An old man with green trousers, grey chest, and white hair. What is it? A snow mountain.'' Or ''an armored soldier, useful only when dead. What is it? Tinned meat.''

In the centuries between these early folk beginnings (which still persist in wedding songs, house-building rounds, idle riddling, juniper offering ceremonies, etc.) and the introduction of metric verses modeled on Indian aesthetics (tenth century C.E.) little is known of the development of the literary arts in Tibet. Apart from lexicographical and annalistic works, one must search hard to find what might have happened. After the extirpation of Buddhism from Central Tibet between 836 and 842 C.E. and the founding of a Buddhist dynasty in Western Tibet in the eleventh century C.E., a new character must have slowly formed as a more personal and yet direct style. This style became the hallmark of a remarkable piece of invective from this later period. Lha Lama Yeshe Od wrote a stinging diatribe against the so-called ''corrupt'' practices which he felt had been allowed to creep unchecked into Buddhism. He shows a masterly use of a truly Tibetan directness and uses images far removed from the limiting confines of the monas-

Printing Prayer Books at Kumbum Monastery.   Photo: Carole Elchert

tic life and the literary style that often grew up around the Mahayana. He said:

> Village abbots, your tantrist way of practicing,
> Will shock if the people of other countries hear of it.
> These practices of you who say, "We are Buddhists"
> Show less compassion than a demon of action.
> More avaricious for meat than a hawk or wolf.
> More lusty than a mere donkey or ox.
> More greedy for beer than a beetle in a rotten house.
> More indifferent to pure and impure than a dog or a pig...²

The great Indian pandita Atisa (982-1054 C.E.) was invited to Tibet from his incumbency as abbot of Vikramasila, one of the most prestigious monastic universities of India, to counter the very practices railed against by Yeshe Od. Atisa's literary output—for example, the renowned *Bodhipathapradipa*—is remarkable for its measured, logical, sequential style. However, as might be expected, this work is thoroughly Indian in character and Mahayanist in tone. Despite the twelve years Atisa spent in Tibet, one has to look hard to find even the smallest vestige of Tibetan influence on his work. However, Atisa's influence on the future of the Tibetans and especially their literature was enormous, and many works bear the imprint of his Indian, Mahayanist format. His influence extended especially to Tsong Khapa (1357-1419 C.E.), whose fully developed Lam Rim style is still used today as a model for other writers wanting to create a predictable, safe, and certain path to enlightenment. One of the most recent and interesting works in this format is the soon-to-be-published work by the great Lama Pabongka Rinpoche, who died in 1947. His work combines this graded aspect with stories from Buddhist legend and Tibetan life to illustrate the path.[3]

Atisa's shadow can also be seen on Gampopa (1079-1153 C.E.), a direct disciple of the hermit/yogin Milarepa. Gampopa's two renowned works, the *Jewel Ornament of Liberation*[4] and the *Jewel Rosary*, might well have been written in India, so thoroughly Mahayanist are they in character. However, from time to time in the latter work, Gampopa slips into a more direct, challenging style—one of the hallmarks of Tibetan writing. He writes tersely in the section entitled ''The Ten Things Which May Be Mistaken For Each Other:''

> Desire may be mistaken for faith.
> Attachment may be mistaken for love and compassion. . . .
> Thought may be mistaken for experience. . . .
> Hypocrites may be mistaken for *siddhas*,
> Those who serve their own interests may be mistaken for altruists.

Another example of this style is found in the chapter entitled ''The Ten Things By Which One Harms Oneself:''

> To be weak-minded and be a lord over men
> Is like an old woman who would be a cattle herder.
> Such a person causes their own harm.
> Beyond all reason, not to strive after the welfare of others,

Prayer Wheels at Tyangboche Monastery.   Ink Drawing—Philip Sugden

And instead to use the eight worldly pursuits for one's own welfare,
Is like a blind person wandering around the icy northern steppes—
Such a person causes their own harm.[5]

    A truly Tibetan Buddhist style of writing can be said to have started again with Marpa the Translator (1011-1098 C.E.), who combined the tantric density of Indian Buddhist literature with frequent and spontaneous imagery of Tibet. Often Marpa used purely local melodies for his songs of realization, and he also extended the Tibetan characteristic for profound and effusive faith in his Guru, making his songs moving and delightful experiences.[6]

    The tantric yogins of Tibet, whether cave-dwelling anchorites such as Milarepa (1040-1121 C.E.), fief-holding vajra-masters such as Marpa, or scholar-yogins such as Padma Karpo (born 1527), mainly set their extemporized songs or other writings to a model of Indian mood or format, but dexterously combined them to a greater (Milarepa) or lesser (Padma Karpo) degree with Tibetan directness, without prevarication or concession. Much imagery was borrowed from the folk-poetry of India, especially Bengal, because sandalwood, deer, elephants, ferryboats, rivers, and lotuses have deep and traditional power as explicators of the tantric mystery.

Milarepa moved much of this imagery to the northern side of the Himalayas and found the same truths explainable in beer-brewing, village life and the mountain environment. Milarepa should not be considered first and foremost as a literary figure, but rather as one who eloquently and passionately described his path towards enlightenment. Indeed, the collections of songs of experience, known as the *One Hundred Thousand Songs*,[7] was not written by Milarepa but by a lineal descendent known as the Bone-Wreathed Yogin Who Haunts Cemeteries, The Mad Yogin of Tsang (1452-1507 C.E.). As is a common practice in Buddhism, these songs were handed down verbatim and finally recorded for posterity when a suitable time and person emerged. One has only to read these wonderful songs to feel a palpable and direct connection with Milarepa's solitary life in the alps. Among soaring eagles, medicinal herbs, and icy rock caverns, he practiced the only path considered worth recording by Tibetans, that of revealing the nature of things as they really are. Milarepa also drew on a particularly old tradition in his advice to his favorite disciple, Rechungpa; he referred to him in terms of the traditional animals which personify the realms of which the sacred land of Tibet was made:

It is good for you, the white lion on the mountain
To stay high and never go deep into the valley,
Lest your beautiful mane be sullied! . . . .
It is good for you, the great
Eagle on high rocks to perch,
And never fall into a pit,
Lest your mighty wings be damaged! . . . .
It is good for you, the jungle tiger,
To stay in the deep forest;
If you rove about the plain
You will lose your dignity. . . .

Pilgrimage to Mt. Kailash.   Oil—John Westmore

It is good for you, the golden-eyed
Fish to swim in the central sea;
If you swim too close to shore,
You will in a net be caught.[8]

A fine article by John Ardussi discusses Milarepa's use of the imagery of beer-brewing, a traditional Tibetan pursuit, as a detail-by-detail analogy for the yogic process towards enlightenment. This is a truly masterly piece of purely Tibetan writing, one in which Indian tantric writers in the centuries before Milarepa would have used the fermentation of wine and the distillation of spirits as their own locally potent set of images.[9]

These charming aspects of Tibetan writing—bringing local color into the main body of the work, if it lacks anything intrinsically Tibetan, or adding minor texts almost as afterthoughts onto one's collected works—continue to this day. Padma Karpo, for example, added at least four pilgrimage guides to collected works. Pawo Tsug (1504-1566) appended a chapter on "general knowledge and the sciences of various lands" to his *History of Buddhism*. Taranatha (born 1575) included chapters on grammar, prosody, pilgrimage guides, and works on some of his great contemporaries. Situ Panchen (1700-1774 C.E.) added chapters on astronomy and astrology according to the Chinese traditions. Sumpa Kenpo (1704-1788 C.E.) wrote minor treatises on world and local geography, divination as it was found in ancient Tibet using heat-cracked sheep scapula, and methods of protection against snow and rain. Longdol Lama (born 1719) included lists of Buddhist patrons, various methods of fortune telling, and even a method of jewel assaying. These examples should dispel any ideas about the ''limitations'' of Tibetan literature; indeed its vitality and scope never cease to amaze. Unfortunately, the vast majority of works by the above-named scholars, among the most eminent of Tibet's savants, have not been translated into English, although at least something is available from them all except Pawo Tsug and Situ Panchen. These writings suggest a deep intellectual ferment in Tibet in those glorious times.[10] Of course, these ''minor'' works included in a written collection were entirely secondary to the raison d'être for the collection, that is, explanation and analysis, description and practice method for the multitude of tantric cycles experienced and meditated on by the authors in their periodic retreats.

However, the lofty writings generally have far less to offer in ''Tibetan-ness'' than the ''secondary'' works even though a vast untapped mine of Tibetan philosophy is developed in such tantric treatises. Among the most venerated of the secondary writings are the histories of Buddhism in India and Tibet, and, in some cases, China and Central Asia. Also included in secondary writings are outstanding summaries of the tenets of the main schools of Buddhist practice and biographies of the lineal predecessors of these schools. Many of these works are carefully reasoned, densely detailed, and use documents not often available to the modern scholar. Many of them remain the best knowledge we have of the transmission of Buddhism to other lands and of the saints and siddhas who exemplified the path to perfection.[11]

I am only too aware that I have entirely omitted any mention of the great Sakya writers of the eleventh to thirteenth centuries C.E., who codified and systematized their entire corpus of doctrines. The Nyingma sect's whole tradition of ''hidden treasure'' writings has not been mentioned, but each of these aspects of the Tibetan literary genius deserves more than a casual mention in a brief survey.

Prayer Book Pages and Dorje.   Photo: Philip Sugden

Readers should discover for themselves the further treasures—level upon level, richness upon richness—in this fruitful and most rewarding field.

Finally, I must mention the profound changes which have emerged in the last thirty or forty years. Foremost among writers who have re-evaluated how Tibetans view their sources of knowledge and the way Tibetans record and write about their history and culture is Gedun Chopel (1905-1951). A peripatetic, prickly, erudite, and inquisitive scholar, Chopel, unlike many of his predecessors, accepted little on precedent and even less on higher authority. Possessed of an unbelievable intellect, he was one of the few lamas to travel outside Tibet to gain knowledge and experience. He flirted with politics and new social viewpoints, passed the British Matriculation degree after studying English for only six months, and easily mastered no fewer than thirteen languages. After delving into unknown sources of Tibetan history, he revealed a richer and more glorious dynastic past than anyone had previously imagined.[12] Chopel translated Indian dramatic works long forgotten in the Land of Snows into Tibetan and aided Roerich in the translation of the *Blue Annals*, a classic Tibetan text, into English.[13] In recent years, his mantle has fallen on many younger scholars who pursue Chopel's goals with equal single-mindedness. Foremost perhaps among these scholars is the great lama, Namkhai Norbu, and his younger confrere, Acharya Tsultrim Kalsang Khangkar. Both are trailblazers as historians who are defining a new and more vital approach to Tibetans' self-definition through scholarship.[14]

The changes that Tibetan literature has undergone since the diaspora of 1959 have been profound, as new influences and vitality course through it. Truly the "Snow Lion" has left its mountain fastness, but far from its mane being sullied, it has grown in stature and dignity. This process of re-evaluation and forthrightness, I hope, will spill over and re-enrich the writers who remain in the Land of Snows so that we may see again all Tibetans working together to create newer and broader horizons.

Notes

1. R. A. Stein, *Tibetan Civilization* (London: Faber and Faber, 1972).

2. Samten Karmay, "The Ordinance of Lha Bla-Ma Ye-Shes-'od," in Aris and Aung, eds., *Tibetan Studies in Honour of Hugh Richardson* (Warminster: Aris and Phillips, 1980).

3. M. Richards, *Liberation in the Palm of Your Hand* (London: Wisdom Publications, forthcoming).

4. H. V. Guenther, *The Jewel Ornament of Liberation* (London: Rider, 1959).

5. Translated from an undated, unlocated manuscript.

6. Nalanda Translation Committee, *The Life of Marpa the Translator* (Boulder: Prajna Press, 1982).

7. Garma C. C. Chang, *The Hundred Thousand Songs of Milarepa*, 2 vols. (Seacaucus: University Books, 1962).

8. Ibid, p. 587.

9. John A. Ardussi, "Brewing and Drinking the Beer of Enlightenment in Tibetan Buddhism: The Doha Tradition in Tibet," *Journal of the American Oriental Society*, 1977.

10. These references are untranslated, so the general reader will not require advice on where they may be found. The reader who speaks Tibetan will find these references in the *dKar chag's* of the authors.

11. For example, Chattopadhyaya, A., *Taranatha's History of Buddhism in India* (Simla: Indian Institute of Advanced Studies, 1970). Obermiller, E., *History of Buddhism by Bu-ston*, 2 vols. (Leipzig: Otto Harrassowitz, 1931-1932).

12. Gedun Choephel, *The White Annals*, trans. Samten Norboo (Dharamsala: Library of Tibetan Works and Archives, 1980).

13. G. Roerich, *The Blue Annals* (reprint ed., Delhi: Motilal Banarsidass, 1976).

14. Namkhai Norbu, *The Necklace of Gzi, A Cultural History of Tibet* (Dharamsala: Information Office of His Holiness the Dalai Lama, 1981). Acharya Tsultrim Kalsang Khangkar, *Tibetan History: "Tibet and Tibetans"* (in Tibetan) (New Delhi: Western Tibetan Cultural Association, 1980).

Buddhist Nuns, Dharamsala.

Photo: Philip Sugden

PART II

Carole at Yarlung.

Journal Entries

Carole Elchert

From a place halfway around the globe, I came home not wanting to tell much, or maybe not knowing what to tell. What about the names and places—you might ask— the details, the ordinary in cultural disguise? There are those particularly joyous times, I answer, that rustle to be told, but all these facets of the experience have little to do with what a person comes to know while traveling. Even if I told you about the circumstances of the trip, you would only know the mirage of my recollections while the journey goes on within me. What I brought home to keep is part of my silence, and there, my knowing stands aloof and unspoken. So, then, what is it I give you when I speak about my journey? I give you the questions you'll ask after I tell my simple stories, and these become your empty spaces. These become the wide expanses of knowing you must cross. My stories may even become that shoreline from which you leave home.

May 5, 1988: Sera Monastery

Today while we walked through the chapels of Sera's two colleges, the main assembly hall, and the monastery grounds, I saw few traces of the four hundred monks who are reported to live and study at Sera. The resounding quiet and the monks' absence felt strange, like a rub in the wrong direction, because Sera is the size of a small township.

At one time Sera was one of the three most influential Gelukpa monasteries with resident populations swelled by monks who came from all areas of Tibet for monastic training and study. Ganden once housed more than five thousand monks. Drepung housed as many as seven thousand, and Sera had five thousand resident monks, novices, and functionaries. During the thirty years that the Communists tried to wring religion out of Tibetans' lives, the monastic population at Sera was considerably reduced by limits on novitiates, harassment, imprisonment, and executions—policies which clearly spelled out Beijing's commitment to the practice of religion.

Most of the morning, expedition members followed pilgrims caked with weeks of travel grime. On their devotional rounds, they dripped melted butter into votive lamps of flickering light. Apart from that small group of pilgrims, I noticed a few monks and great numbers of sleeping dogs. I joked with Phuntsok, our Tibetan guide and translator, that Sera's reputation as a humane institution for all sentient beings had gotten around, since the monastery apparently housed nine hundred dogs and only four hundred monks. Phuntsok laughed, but not because he appreciated my humor. More likely, he laughed from an irony jabbing him hard in the ribs. Shortly thereafter, we stepped over a sleeping dog and came to a door that a monk had just locked. The monk shrugged when we asked to go inside, and after he slipped away, Phuntsok blurted out that someday he would go to India, and he would enter a monastery there.

May 7, 1988: Lhasa's Jokhang Temple: written on site

Outside the Jokhang Temple in the early evening, I sit with my eyes closed and listen to the shuffling sounds of the prostrators. Unconcerned with my presence, about thirty people in the front courtyard of the "Lord's House," the literal meaning of Jokhang, move through the ritual of prostration. Folded hands touch foreheads and hearts before prostrators fall to their knees and then lie full-length on the cobbled pavement or sometimes on mats that protect their bodies. As the prostrators rise and fall with tireless devotion, it is easy to get caught up in the rhythm and labored breathing of their piety.

This evening, a young Tibetan woman is teaching a two-year-old how to prostrate. The child can barely walk upright without that first-step wobble, but the small hands have already been taught to fold themselves. Playing to an adult audience which beams reassurance, the boy is delighted to fold his hands and allow his mother to press his body into the face-down, full-length position. Over and over, the mother and child repeat this act, the boy's clumsy movements forming a lifetime habit that age might stiffen but does not discourage. Most of the thirty or more prostrators are older people—all of whom are committed to an exhausting repetition that I've only seen in the worship of toned muscles we in the West call aerobics.

Before I leave my nightly post near the prostrators, I check the time and realize that my watch is confusing the issue. In fact, more time is passing than a watch ever admits. All times are present and all ages, too. A mother instructing a child was the past for all the prostrating adults. In the midst of this past, the future is also being acted out in front of my eyes; the child's future is the aged habits of devotion of all these adults. As I watch the prostrators rise and fall like the breath of the living, I think about the childhood memories of Tibetans, one of the strongest of which is imprinted when a mother first bends a child's torso and volition low. And I understand how children become the adults, then, who bend and stretch a hundred thousand times toward a reality that can only be known if the ego is guided low.

May 11, 1988: Lake Namtso

I walked with Jigme, our first Tibetan guide, on the beach of Drarshido (pronounced "Tashido"). Drarshido, an immense red monolith rising from a broad plain like Australia's Ayers Rock, protected us from the fierce winds at 15,000 feet that created six-foot whitecaps on Tibet's largest salt lake.

Accompanying us was a nomad girl. Unbelievably she had followed a vehicle track to Drarshido on a plain, a week's walk in length, that appeared featureless to my eye. The girl wore a scarf around her face for protection from winds that never ceased and dust that never settled on the treeless Chang Tang plains. While she recounted local legends about the ancient hermitages tucked into the base of the Drarshido fortress, Jigme—who had told me when we met that his parents were Shigatse nobility and that, in addition to Tibetan, he spoke fluent Chinese—seemed to be having difficulty speaking with the girl. The girl spoke softly and in short phrases that barely sustained conversation. Even though she was as eager to talk as she was to help us find our way, Jigme's face was pinched with his efforts to communicate.

Finally, Jigme turned to me and apologized for having difficultly understanding the girl. He said that the nomads speak a strange dialect, a low form of the Tibetan language—a remark in character for someone who identifies with a noble birth. I knew that the nomads, numbering one half of the six million Tibetans on the plateau, speak a dialect associated with their region of birth. And I speak very little Tibetan, the scant phrases of necessity, but I replied as though I'd achieved instant realization: ''Well, no wonder I couldn't understand a word she said.'' Like most Tibetans, his laugh was a cloudburst, and like most Tibetans who don't speak a word of English but know a good joke when they hear it, the nomad girl laughed, too.

May 20, 1988: Samye Monastery

Samye Monastery is located at the foot of Hepori, one of the four holiest mountains in Tibet. Tibet's first Buddhist monastery built in the eighth century C.E. was framed by a valley green with the spring planting of barley. While I took photographs, a young girl followed me around the ruins of Kamsam Saggak Ling. Once a thriving monastic building, it is now the living quarters of farmers who tend the area fields. The girl was dragging a white calf on a leash as she watched me photograph murals whose images were somehow scratched off courtyard walls. She smiled, nodding ''yes'' when I gestured how a pick or shovel might have caused the damaged. Although the walls were all painted with murals, their vibrancy could only be seen in patches that survived the bleaching of time. Of the murals assaulted by the Cultural Revolution's Red Guard frenzy, the one most often a silhouette in cement on the faded background of scenic landscape was that of the Buddha.

Inside, the courtyard had the peeling atmosphere of decay. Only thirty years ago monks lived, prayed, and studied in a courtyard that was not the girl's playground—a playground occupied by farm implements, wagons, livestock, piles of discarded tire rims, and junk stacked on junk. I've seen plants decompose for years and woods littered with ice-storm damage, but I've never felt that these natural processes of decay and change were unsightly. However, the rusting metal and rubber tires in careless piles desecrated the face of this ancient monastery, which was mostly the work of artists and craftsmen. Taking in the scene, I felt as though an auto mechanic had opened a body shop in the Sistine Chapel where he stored discarded parts because there was all this empty space. Scrap was thrown around capriciously, as if the mechanic had them thrown buckets of paint on the walls of the Chapel because there was nowhere else to put the old paint.

The atmosphere of the courtyard held anticipation, too. The assembly hall, where monks once met for daily *puja* (prayer) services, was locked. Even though the present was kept at bay, the locks also ensured a future for this place. The large Tibetan locks on the doors not only kept intruders out, but also invited the future to fling open its doors again someday. On the entrance walls, images of the four protector deities are still on duty. But now they are faded and patchy versions of their once vivid representation of guardianship from the North, South, East, and West. In English, I asked the girl which deity was on guard duty when the Chinese army bludgeoned a path across Tibet in the '50s, but she answered in Tibetan, so I'll never know.

The girl followed me around the courtyard, pulling the calf behind her. A ten-foot pile of discarded tire rims reminded me of Tibetans' ancient legend that forecast the destruction of their culture when "the wheel turns and the iron bird flies." Before 1950 the most common wheel in Tibet was the hand-held prayer wheel rotated to gain spiritual merit. As I framed to photograph the rubble of technology, the girl and her unleashed white calf started to climb the pile.

Later that day the girl was bringing the yak-cow crossbred called a *dzo* in from pasture. When she spotted me walking toward our tent site on the littered picnic grounds around the monastery, she smiled and waved giddily, and I smiled too, like a favored playmate. She turned away, though, when she saw a blue-uniformed and, therefore, very official Chinese woman eyeing us from the roadside. From a distance the woman scolded the girl, perhaps for the indiscretion of friendliness. The girl hurried past the woman's scowl, and once out of official sight, she looked back at me and silently mouthed "goodbye" in English. I answered quietly in Tibetan, *kaliy shu*, which is the wish that she "carefully stay." As the person staying behind, the girl responded, *kaliy pay*, which literally means "carefully go." In these two common forms of goodbye I was never more certain that the meaning of goodbye was completely understood.

May 21, 1988: Yarlung Tsangpo River

The day was exquisite for a drive. The gravel road we were traveling followed the sandbar-slackened course of the Yarlung Tsangpo. For eight hundred miles the river crosses the Central Tibetan Plateau, but only after it descends through Himalayan escarpments to the plains of India does this 1,800-mile river achieve worldwide status and fame as the sacred Brahmaputra. Here in Tibet, the cobalt blue river courses through the brown and grey hues of a parched land. Beyond the snaking blueness of the Tsangpo River and the serried hills is a sky bluer still, and, having seen all this, I think that any sober person would choose the intoxication of knowing and having the blues in Tibet.

The drive was maddening for a view. All morning I tried to photograph between telephone poles that pare the wide and spacious landscape into blocks and chunks of insubstantial views. What is most frustrating about any form of transportation in Tibet other than "hoofing it"—your own or the hoof of some less stubborn animal—is that you're always told that the vehicle must be at so-and-so by such-and-such a time because towns and villages are considerable distances apart. The driver, of course, is motivated to get there, but passengers are then frustrated in their need to be "here." Between there and here for driver and traveler is the vast plateau, fragmented and framed by telephone poles that don't have the aesthetic sense to hide themselves.

Only thirty years ago, a journey across Tibet offered the travel wide-angle servings of vast, desolate, untamed, and quieting land. But now that the tall poles of somebody else's interpretation of progress have partitioned the landscape of Tibet, the viewer is left hungering for an expansiveness which is a rare feast today.

May 26, 1988: Rongbuck Monastery at the base of Mt. Everest

If any country were to apply for wilderness status from border to border, this capacious land would certainly qualify. On 500,000 square miles of mostly inhospitable terrain, Tibetan villages are great distances apart. So today on a rugged stretch of back country, I was sure I'd see some of the wildlife indigenous to these remote highlands. We'd traveled overland for three weeks, and in the great distances I never saw the gazelle, chiru (antelope), kyang, bighorn sheep, wolf, fox, or musk deer that were sighted in great numbers by British and German explorers in the '20s, '30s, and '40s. Suddenly, when a gazelle jumped from the camouflage of brown hills, we were startled, and a sound like pity escaped our lips as it bounded across the empty plateau made emptier still by its solidary presence.

For several hours we bounced across terrain that rearranges bones in the body. We passed a ridge, and all four of us yelled simultaneously for the jeep to stop. Even though our rear ends had collided with the seat for an entire morning, four bone-weary passengers burst from the jeep for the pain of a staggering view. Before us was Rongbuck Monastery at the base of Mt. Everest. As though to take the most prominent seat in a valley amphitheater, the *gompa* (monastery) was built on a hillside facing the highest mountain on earth. In the traditional Tibetan manner of high rise architecture, Rongbuck's walls sloped upward and inward, emulating the massive, granite spire of Mt. Everest, which rises from the glaciated valley a day's distance away.

Rongbuck is the highest monastery on earth. In Rongbuck's windswept backyard 29,000 foot Mt. Everest stands as the highest neighbor. I believe, however, that size and scale have little to do with the effect of this place. Except for the monastery's whitewashed walls, the gutted ruins of Cultural Revolution chaos, a few stone huts, and the frozen white face of Mt. Everest, the land is desolate and spare. I was overwhelmed by a landscape stripped down to sky, mountain, and whitewashed gompa walls. I wanted to rest there in the valley's empty-handedness, to do nothing but watch and wait—as the Rongbuck monks and nuns do—for nothing much to happen.

In this valley where no one doubts that the mountain is a god, something is about to happen, though, something the architect of Rongbuck Gompa must have known was in the original stakes when he selected the site. The view from Rongbuck is unparalleled. Translated into outcomes in a modern world, the monastery sits on prime ground for two nations to parlay the moutainview. Phuntsok (our Tibetan guide) explained China and Nepal's proposal to create a binational park of the area surrounding the north and south face of Mt. Everest. Their plan would protect what remained of the decimated wildlife, while regulating the thousands of tourists and climbers expected annually and the additional trekkers who would circle the mountain from Thami, Nepal. I wondered, though, how generally unsociable wildlife, like the elusive snow leopard, fit into a scheme that opens the territories where they range to migrating tour groups.

I thought about the road that would tame the journey to this holy mountain; I imagined the great migration of bus, jeep, and truck traffic. With hotels and restaurants serving tourists what they've become accustomed to—comforts and regular tea service—the valley that exalts the mountain will certainly be made more accommodating. But will the place remain a pilgrimage site? When Mt. Everest is finally staked off as a preserve, and it will be developed as just another piece of mountainside real estate, the losses and gains will be high. What is most likely to be preserved, though, is a euphemism, a cosmeticized experience, and the "holy travail" will be removed from travel to the sacred mountain.

On the last evening at Rongbuck Monastery, walled in luxurious silence by Mt. Everest—which to Tibetans is Chomolungma, "Mother Goddess of the World"—I wondered if the great bands of tourists to come would take the trouble to return to the holy mountain as pilgrims. A view, after all, is no trouble for a traveler to take home on a postcard.

May 28, 1988: Nyelam—Milarepa's cave

Sometimes a glance, a few casual words, fragments of a melody floating through the quiet air of a summer evening, a book that accidentally comes into our hands, a poem or a memory-laden fragrance, may bring about the impulse which changes and determines our whole life.

—Lama Govinda, The Way of the White Clouds

The expedition's good luck wasn't dispensing its favors as usual. The caretaker monk had left for the day, so we could only peer into Milarepa's cave through a cracked window. Milarepa, the cave-dwelling mystic who composed insights into songs, would have been pleased with our fate. Namkha Ding, which means "hovering in space," was Milarepa's poetic name for his cave retreat. What better place to find idle time and the surcease of plans than outside a locked door, a thought which seemed to poke fun at my irritation.

When I turned to leave, I bumped into a Tibetan girl holding a basket. She offered me the basket, and when I reached inside, my hand felt the unforgettable sting of fresh-picked nettles. I looked around to see which sage-prankster had choreographed this joke, since Milarepa is usually pictured with a green complexion—the result, apparently of his ascetic diet of nettles.

While chewing nettles—frankly, the coincidence was unnerving—the girl and a friend held my hands and guided me across the hills that afternoon. They escorted me on steep trails wide enough for a goat's hoof and across waterfalls of spring snowmelt as though I was fragile and old. They led me on a narrow path to flowering trees and shrubs, and there, they insisted I taste the blossoms. I chewed on the sweet-tasting stems they handed me, and I drank water from a cupped leaf. Being younger than I and many years closer to the earth, they didn't let me pass a thing to get somewhere; we tasted, smelled, held and examined, stumbled into and climbed over everything on our path. For an entire afternoon I ingested, sometimes more literally than I wanted to, whatever there was to experience and absorbed the implications of such living through every pore.

By the end of our walk, I didn't feel certain about many things I knew before, but I felt certain of several things I doubted before. Every mundane thing we'd done could fill an idle afternoon or occupy a lifetime, as it must have for the sage-poet, Milarepa. I had no doubts that these two girls had guided me through the routine of a man—more spirit than tissue—who once lived and walked on these steep mountainsides. And I knew what I no longer doubted, that idleness is the welcome mat before the door of most sacred places. That is where we are precariously "hovering in the space" between doing nothing and realizing everything while doing nothing.

When they waved goodbye and I swallowed hard the last bit of a woody stem,

I asked myself, "How do you ever know a closed door wasn't the best thing you came upon that day?"

May 28, 1988: Khasa at the Tibet/Nepal border

Khasa (Zhamu on Chinese maps) is the end of the line for traveler on the over-land route from Lhasa to Nepal. Khasa is a glum place to spend an evening. There, it is possible to spend a lifetime of desultory minutes after only one hour. The town streets, if not the atmosphere, are muddy even on a sunny day, and people seem a little uncomfortable, as though they are only visiting the place. Shops and homes seem like places where no one ever answers the door.

Adding to the complication and irritation of life in Khasa, traders and busi-nesses operate as if three different time zones exist within the town's boundaries. The Nepalese follow Kathmandu time. Kathmandu time is a languourous three hours behind Beijing time, which, despite the sun's position on the matter, pre-vails over the whole of China proper (the width of four time zones). And the Tibetans lag behind the official Beijing time by one surly hour. We discovered these discrepancies when we arranged a ride with a truck heading back to Kath-mandu. A Nepalese trader suggested that we meet at 7:30 a.m. "Kathmandu standard time," he added. At that time, the customs checkpost would be open-ing its doors—10:30 a.m. Beijing time. We ended up catching a ride, though, with a group of Tibetans who arrived on time for the borders to open at 11:30 a.m., Tibetan standard time.

Time wasn't the only thing askew in this border town.

Khasa is a town where everyone is gone or waiting to go someplace else. John (the Australian painter who also paints with words) says of the atmosphere: "It's like a bloody bus stop without the buses running." People are most often "just in" from somewhere or delayed for weeks from going on to someplace else. Many small-statured Nepalese traders arrive here for a few hours or several days to sell the goods of a more temperate climate. Many young Tibetans—taller, big-boned, weathered, and worked lean—are here for the heavy loading and unloading of trucks. And then there are the Chinese. They seem most at odds with the place and look over their shoulders at the other two groups: the fiercely enterprising

Nepalese and the fiercely congenial Tibetans, who seem most at home with all the strangers in their land. The Chinese, like the one who caught me waving at him through his binoculars, watch everything with an unveiled suspicion, probably because they and their suspicions are not native to this land.

The Chinese soldier finally realized that I was waving at him while he was spying on me, and he backed away, red-faced and smiling. He had been caught in the act, and his embarrassment was an open confession. When he crossed to the other side of his inherited cultural reserve and waved back, I knew then that travelers, like myself, were going to conquer the conquerors of Tibet. We'll just watch them while they watch us. Then we'll go home with stories a lens-eye closer to the truth, with hands raised and waving in support of the truth. In homes and in auditoriums and in the words on a page, we'll take the witness stand because diplomats and journalists under the restraints of martial law are not allowed to stand in Tibet's defense. These days, ordinary travelers, but only as ordinary as a monsoon downpour on a desert day, must bear witness, and then the conquest of an Autonomous Region not yet autonomous will begin to end.

Young Tibetan at Shalu Monastery, Tibet.   Photo: Carole Elchert

Photo: Carole Elchert

Pendant le voyage ma flute ne me quittait pas. L'étendue du paysage, les merveilleuses couleurs m'inspiraient pour composer. Les Tibetans, respectueux et spirituels, me donnaient une grande confiance et un grand épanouissement par leurs nombreaux rites. Ils aident à trouver l'harmonie avec les gens et a découvrir l'environnement.

Prelude Aulde Lelarge

Aulde Lelarge

During the trip I carried my flute everywhere, in the rain, in the cold, or in the sun. The open spaces, the gigantic mountains, the immense valleys, the special wonderful color gave me a lot of inspiration to compose. Tibetans have much respect for others; they listen without disturbing. They gave me confidence and warm emotions to translate into notes. The rituals, which involve many people, send out intense vibrations and help the participants be in harmony with other people and with the environment. Mystery, gladness, and birds dancing everywhere create a wonderful, deep emotion.

A *Guide to the Video* White Lotus

Background

The unifying theme of the video is conveyed by its title, *White Lotus*, and what this concept represents to the Tibetan people. This name is the literal English rendering of *Padma Karpo*, a title suggested by Tibetan scholars in Dharamsala, India.

Padma is a Sanskrit term meaning lotus (flower). The lotus symbolizes what all humans can ultimately achieve, enlightenment. Enlightenment then is the lotus flower that raises itself above an ordinary world muddied by such ubiquitous miseries as suffering, loss, change, and deterioration. All physical life is rooted in a muddied existence, and all hope for eventual release through enlightenment is also rooted in the same context.

Karpo is the Tibetan word for white, the color that suggests the purity and clarity which contrasts the mire of life. In the historical flowering of the Tibetan culture, which is older than 2,000 years, what is most pure like ''the jewel in the center of the lotus flower'' is the Tibetan's religion, Mahayana Buddhism. Mahayana Buddhist philosophy and symbols underlie the Tibetan's daily rituals and fashion many aspects of their material culture.

The visual images for the video were selected from 20,000 slides photographed by P. Sugden, C. Elchert, and R. Sugden during the 1988 Cultural Arts Expedition and a 1989 journey by Elchert to Eastern Tibet. The audio portion of the video includes C. Elchert's field recordings of traditional and environmental sounds native to the Tibetans' everyday lives. While revealing literal aspects of the Tibetans' culture, the video also recreates an experience of sights and sounds.

Video Sequences:

The video opens with the title, *Padma Karpo*, in Tibetan script, and then its literal English translation appears. In a series of continuous sequences, the video conveys information pictorially about some of the issues that define Tibetan culture: environment, architecture, monastic life, art and symbology, shrines, domestic life, and ethnic characteristics.

1. Environment: For most of its history until the Chinese invasion in the 1950s, Tibet remained isolated from the world by several mountain ranges and the vast, bitter-cold desert areas of the Chang Tang plateau. Opening scenes of the Himalaya—the Sanskrit term meaning "snow abode"—establish a sense of place. Most of Tibet lies at altitudes above 12,000 feet. Images of this mountainous landscape also convey a sense of the mystery, the mystical quality ascribed to high places. Images also reveal the vastness of the Chang Tang landscape. The Central Plateau in winter is an isolated, austere vastness. Signs of life—yaks, a few flat-roofed homes—appear fragile and dwarfed by expanding distances. The final images show the variation in seasons and climate. Central Tibet includes agricultural land along the Yarlung Tsangpo River. Much of the Tibetan plateau, however, is arid, sparse pastureland used to graze animals (primarily yaks, sheep, and goats). In the Eastern Tibetan region of Amdo, now a part of Qinghai Province, lush fir forests and fertile terraced hillsides exist in sharp contrast with the predominately drier regions of the Central Plateau.

2. Architecture: The visual focus changes subtly, from an emphasis on land to man-made structures in the landscape. This sequence reveals a close relationship between architecture and the land. From rock formations having an architectural quality to small shrines (*chortens*) and ancient forts that follow the contour of the mountainsides, images suggest a consonance between architecture and the physical attributes of Tibet's mountainous, rock and desert terrain. Side-by-side dis-solving images of mountains and monasteries show how stone and mud-brick ar-chitecture copies nature, and how the environment dictates structure. In the arid Central Plateau, most homes are flat-roofed, but the deeper topsoil of the eastern uplands is used to build stacked sod homes. In Eastern Tibet, rooftops are ga-bled because of the heavier rainfall of subtropical conditions. A closer inspection of the decorative and functional aspects of Tibetan architecture is achieved through a series of abrupt visual cuts initiated by the sounds of conch shells and Tibetan horns—instruments used in monastic ritual.

3. Monastic Life: Monks are shown responding to the horns and moving toward monastery entrances. Images show the exteriors of many monasteries from areas in Tibet (Labrang, Kumbum, Drigung, Tashilhunpo) and in India (Sera). En-trance gates (Samye) and one of the four guardian deities painted on the outside walls direct attention toward interiors of temples and monasteries. Inside candle-lit hallways, images reveal the muted colors of frescoes. Chanting can be heard from a distant prayer room within a monastery. On the final climactic beat of a *damaru* drum, a blast of ritual sounds initiates a sequence of images that fo-cuses on monastic ritual and worship.

4. Art: The artwork that was incidental in the monastic sequence becomes the visual focus. Sculpture, *thangka* (scroll) paintings, and frescoes are visual sources of cultural information. Tibetan art presents aspects of religious beliefs, cultural values, and historical events through representational imagery (the historical Bud-dha) and symbols (the lotus flower, which symbolizes enlightenment). In an at-tempt to familiarize and not necessarily inform, images of artwork are shown as isolated pieces emphasizing their aesthetic beauty and shown in the context of the monastic setting. Primary colors on interior walls, ceilings, pillars, and the wooden frames of doors and windows contrast sharply with the subdued earth tones of the Central Plateau.

5. Shrines: The vibrant primary and secondary colors seen in interior frescoes are also used on exterior walls of temples and on prayer wheels (*korlo*). These prayer-filled drums are spun by pilgrims who follow a traditional clockwise path around temples and monasteries. With each rotation, thousands of sacred mantras printed on paper rolls inside the drum are offered by the pilgrim and, in return, the pilgrim gains spiritual merit.

Like the prayer wheels, *mani* (prayer) stones and *chortens* (shrines) are vehicles of prayer as well as cultural symbols. These significant religious structures are usually located on prominent sites (high passes) and pilgrim routes. Walls and flat beds of mani stones, which are carved and sometimes painted with prayers, surround Tibetan communities and monasteries. When travelers or pilgrims inscribe prayers on wayside rocks or place stones in pyramid forms, impromptu shrines are created. These small mounds of piled stones mirror the more formal chorten, which is the distinctive reliquary shrine found throughout those areas where Tibetan Buddhism was practiced. Shaped like an overturned bowl with a spire on top—ancient, nearly decomposed ''chortens'' and the more recent constructions represent levels of human existence.

6. Domestic Life: From a community of shrines, the scene moves to a village where a chorten, like the Buddhist religion, occupies a central position in Tibetans' domestic life. Images show the flat rooftops where much household life occurs. Inside a home, a room is scanned, and its sparse contents used for cooking, farming, sleeping, and worship are shown. A Tibetan woman roasts barley kernels to prepare the flour called *tsampa*, the staple of the Tibetans' high altitude diet. From inside a home and then from the courtyard, images depict domestic activities, including the sorting and drying of grain and vegetables. Humans and yaks are shown portering water and supplies. The yak, the most important domesticated animal of the high Tibetan plateau, is the beast of burden for agriculture. A series of images shows fields being plowed and seeded, crops being harvested, and fodder being hauled for sheep and goats. The final images present nomadic life on the plateau in summer and winter conditions. Over one-third of Tibet's population is involved in raising livestock, which includes yaks, sheep, goats, and horses.

7. Ethnic Characteristics: The Tibetan people are the subject of this final visual and audio montage. A close-up of a shepherdess's face introduces a series of over one hundred images of Tibetan individuals. Ornamentation, hair-style, and dress distinguish the various ethnic groups from different regions, including the Tibetans of the Central Plateau, Amdo, Kham, Ladakh, and those now living in exile in India and Nepal.

Images of faces dissolve at a progressively faster rate, climaxing abruptly on an image of His Holiness the Dalai Lama, the revered spiritual and temporal leader of the Tibetan people. The montage of native sounds also stops at that point, and a low overtone chant begins. The image of the Dalai Lama slowly dissolves into that of Chenrezig, the Tibetans' symbol of compassion. Tibetans see the Dalai Lama as the incarnated and living manifestation of compassion, which is the pivotal theme of Mahayana Buddhism.

White Lotus Fresco, Kumbum Chorten, Tibet.   Photo: Philip Sugden

White Lotus video cassette offer:

A video cassette of White Lotus is available from WBGU-TV. If you are interested in ordering a copy, contact:

> White Lotus vhs Tape Offer
> WBGU-TV
> 245 Troup Street
> Bowling Green, Ohio 43403

or telephone (419) 372-2700. The video cassette is available for personal or instructional use only. No admission charge or duplication of the program is permitted.

Biographies of Expedition Members

Philip Sugden, co-organizer of the Cultural Arts Expedition, was educated at the New York School of Visual Arts and the Paris American Academie des Beaux Arts. His works of art, based on six journeys to the Himalayas and Tibet, have been exhibited in galleries and museums throughout the world, including

Artist Philip Sugden Drawing at Ganden Monastery, Tibet.   Photo: Carole Elchert

Paris, London, New York, Los Angeles, and Kathmandu. He is currently a part-time instructor in The University of Findlay's Fine Arts Department.

Co-organizer of the Cultural Arts Expedition, **Carole Elchert** writes short stories, essays, and nonfiction based on five trips to the Himalayas.

Writer Carole Elchert Recording at Nechung Monastery, Dharamsala.   Photo: Philip Sugden

Currently an Assistant Professor of Communication at The University of Findlay, she also ghostwrites, edits manuscripts, and provides consulting assistance in group process for area businesses. Elchert holds a Master of Arts in Communication from Bowling Green State University and was awarded an ''Artist In Residence'' grant from the Ohio Arts Council. Her Cibachrome prints have been exhibited in New York, Los Angeles and London.

Flutist Aulde Lelarge Composing in the Himalayas.
Photo: Carole Elchert

Artist John Westmore Drawing in Tibet.
Photo: Carole Elchert

Aulde Lelarge was born in France and currently resides in Paris. As a flutist, she was trained at the Paris Municipal Conservatory under the guidance of Rampal's teacher and student. Presently, she improvises and composes her own work and teaches music in nursery and elementary schools.

Australian artist, **John Westmore**, studied painting at the Royal Melbourne Institute of Technology, the Paris American Academie des Beaux Arts, and Marylebone Institute, London. After travels to Europe and the Himalaya regions and exhibitions in Australia and overseas, Westmore held his first solo exhibition in 1989 at the University of Melbourne. He was an organizer of Tibet Himalaya Festival at the Royal Exhibition Hall, Melbourne.

Roger Sugden first photographed while in Vietnam in 1970. When he returned to the U.S., he acquired a Bachelor of Fine Arts in photography from The University of Central Florida. His photographs are in the permanent collection of the Chrysler Museum, Virginia. In addition to having works published in such magazines as *Venture Inward, Camera*

35, *Style* and *Homes*, Sudgen created a slide essay about Richmond, Virginia, for *Time Life Books*. His work also appears in *The Best of Photography Annual* for 1989.

Biographies of the Contributing Writers

José Ignacio Cabezón is an Assistant Professor at the Iliff School of Theology in Denver, Colorado. Author of several texts and articles on Indo-Tibetan Buddhist thought, Cabezón lived among the Tibetans in India for five years and has served as an interpreter for His Holiness the Dalai Lama.

Photographer Roger Sugden at Bodhnath. Photo: Philip Sugden

    Nima Dorjee was born in Kham Province, East Tibet, and left Tibet in 1959 during the Tibetan uprising against Chinese occupation. He was educated at Rato Monastery, Lhasa, and at Sanskrit University, Varanasi, India, in history, philosophy, language, and the cultures of Tibet and India. He came to the U.S. in 1969. With a research grant from the Rockefeller Foundation, he will complete a book on the history and culture of Dagyab State, Kham. He has also acted as a consultant to the Newark Museum and private art collectors. Since 1985, he has been employed at the Jacques Marchais Center of Tibetan Art.

    With a Ph.D. in the History of Religions from The University of Chicago, **Gary L. Ebersole** is currently an Assistant Professor in the Department of East Asian Languages and Literatures at The Ohio State University. He is an Associate in The Center for Comparative Studies in the Humanities, where he is Director of the Religious Studies Program. With a background in both South Asian Studies and Japanese Studies, his research interests have focused on such topics as the ritual uses of poetry, the interplay of narrative structure, interpretive paradigms and cultural change, and the socio-political and religious dimensions of oral performative poetry. Professor Ebersole frequently reviews books for *Religious Studies Review*, *The Journal of Religion*, *Choice*, *The Journal of Ritual Studies*, *The East-*

ern Buddhist, and other academic journals.

Claude Philippe d'Estrée, M.T.S., J.D., continued to teach at Harvard Divinity School after receiving his degree in Comparative Religion in 1980. In 1982 he was appointed the first Buddhist Lopon (Chaplain) at Harvard University by His Holiness the Dalai Lama. He has also taught at Northeastern University School of Law and at Interface Foundation. Recently he was appointed Lecturer at The University of Arizona. His current work focuses on comparative spiritual disciplines and the role of religion in international conflict resolution.

Born in Kandze, East Tibet, **Lopsang Geleg** holds a Ph.D. in Anthropology form Zhungshan University in Guangzhou, China. Currently he is an Associate Professor and Director of the Institute of Socio-historical Studies of the Chinese Center for Tibetological Studies. He has written monographs and more than twenty scholarly papers on aspects of Tibetan history and culture.

Anne Klein teaches in the Department of Religious Studies at Rice University, Texas. She holds a Ph.D. in Religious Studies from the University of Virginia where she specialized in Tibetan Buddhism. She has also studied with leading Geluk and Nyingma scholars in India and Nepal. Professor Klein is author of *Knowledge and Liberation, Knowing, Naming and Negation*, and numerous articles on women, Buddhism, and the history of religion.

Nancy E. Levine has a Ph.D. in Anthropology and is currently an Associate Professor at the University of California, Los Angeles. She conducted three and a half years of field research among agricultural populations in the Tibetan-speaking northern borderlands of Nepal. Her research and writings have focused on kinship, marriage, family systems, population dynamics, and ethnic relations. Her most recent book is entitled *The Dynamics of Polyandry: Kinship, Domesticity, and Population on the Tibetan Border*.

Born and brought up in Lhasa where he received a secular and monastic education, **Lobsang Lhalungpa** studied under many eminent lamas of various Tibetan Buddhist orders. He served on the staff of the Dalai Lama's Grand Secretariat in the Potala Palace. In India, he was Tibet's cultural envoy for years, a Buddhist teacher, and the director of the Tibetan Radio broadcasts in Delhi. Once the Dalai Lama set up his government-in-exile in India, Lobsang Lhalungpa assisted His Holiness in organizing a new Tibetan educational system, preparing textbooks, and resettling many religious communities in India. After 1970, Lhalungpa taught Buddhism at several Western institutions and wrote numerous articles for international journals. His books include *The Life of Milarepa*, *Tibet, the Sacred Realm*, and *Mahamudra: The Quintessence of Mind and Meditation.*

Barbara Lipton, Director of the Jacques Marchais Center of Tibetan Art in Staten Island, New York, has degrees from the University of Iowa and The University of Michigan in English Literature and Oriental Art History. She has organized many exhibitions for museums in the United States and for the Canadian government. Previously employed at the Newark Museum and the Castle Gallery of the College of New Rochelle, Mrs. Lipton is author of numerous catalogs and articles on Eskimos of Alaska and Canada. She is co-author of *Westerners in Tibet*, published by the Newark Museum. She has also traveled frequently in the Himalayan region.

Donald S. Lopez, Jr. is a Professor of Buddhist Studies at The University of Michigan in the Department of Asian Languages and Cultures. He received his Ph.D. in Buddhist Studies from the University of Virginia.

Molly McGinn studied Buddhism in Japan for over three years. She has taught at Doshisha Women's College in Kyoto, Chengdu University of Science and Technology in China, and Tibet Teachers' College in Lhasa. McGinn is a writer, photographer, and lecturer on Tibet. Her doctoral work in anthropology at UCLA focuses on monasticsm in Tibet. She also develops cross-cultural programs for United Airlines.

After studying Tibetan Buddhism in Dharamsala, India, **David Templeman** returned to his home in Australia, where he is presently the director of Tibet Information Service. Templeman has translated several books on aspects of Tibetan Buddhism, including *The Origin of the Tara Tantra*, *The Seven Instruction Lineages*, and *The Life of Kanha.* He has written numerous articles for such Buddhist journals as *Evam* and *The Tibet Journal.*

Professor **Robert A. F. Thurman** was educated at Harvard University and studied extensively under His Holiness the Dalai Lama and other learned Tibetan masters. He has spent many years doing extensive research and teaching Buddhist Studies. An authority in Indology, Tibetology, and Buddhology, Professor Thurman has published numerous books and essays. Currently he teaches in the

Department of Religion at Columbia University and serves as President of the American Institute of Buddhist Studies.

Marilyn Robinson Waldman is currently a Professor of Islamic History and the Director of the Center for Comparative Studies in the Humanities at The Ohio State University. Professor Waldman holds a Ph.D. in Islamic History from the University of Chicago and has published many books and articles on Islamic history, historiography, and the history of religions. Vice-president of the American Society for the Study of Religion, Professor Waldman has also been a active public speaker on topics related to religious studies and cross-cultural understanding.

Stephen White was educated at Washington University, St. Louis, where he received degrees in architecture (A.B. and Masters of Architecture). On a Fellowship from the National Endowment for the Humanities, he did graduate study in literature and history. He has worked in architectural offices in San Francisco, St. Louis, Amsterdam, London, and New Delhi. He is currently a visiting Assistant Professor of Architecture at Washington University. With support from the Ford Foundation, he is writing a book (*Building in the Garden*) about American architect, Joseph Allen Stein, who, in addition to practicing in New Delhi since 1952, has worked to protect the cultural heritage and natural environment of the Himalaya.

In 1982, **Gary Wintz** and his spouse, Molly McGinn, became the first Westerners to reside in Tibet after the Communist invasion in the '50s. After teaching in Lhasa, they traveled through many remote and forbidden areas of Kham. Wintz currently works in Tibet as a consultant-adviser on Western media, development, and travel projects. He is a writer, photographer, lecturer, and tour director not only in Tibet, but in other Tibetan Buddhist regions of Central Asia, such as Mongolia and Siberia.

Acknowledgements

Video and Companion Book Production

Bob Calmus: Technical and Photographic Assistant
Dave Randles: Design Advisor
Tim Story: Soundtrack Producer and Engineer
Soundtrack Edited and Produced at Scharren Recording Studios, Toledo, Ohio
Sonam Tashi: Instrumental Music
Denise Kisabeth: Director-Editor of the Video Production
Paul Lopez: Videographer
Fred Dickenson: Project Technical Director
Alex Hann: Audio Recording Advisor
Dr. Paul Beauvais: Technical Advisor
Dr. Lynnette Porter: Assistant Editor
Elizabeth Pierce: Assistant Editor
James N. Smith: Assistant Editor
Marji Schott: Assistant Editor
Scott Mulrane: Assistant Editor
Eric Reed: Assistant Editor
Andrea VanVorhis: Assistant Editor
James Greenwood: Assistant Editor

Paula Davis: Promotion, WBGU TV
Anne Miller: Translation
Kathleen Creasy: Musical Arranger
K. M. R. Graphics, Findlay, Ohio
Richard Brumbaugh and Marla K. Vangeloff
B. and J. Photo, Findlay, Ohio
Scott Barker: Photographic Assistance

Secretarial:

Kathy Bradford
Joan Nichols
Mary Pneuman
Jennifer Corner
Eric Schumm
Betty Bozo
Diane McWethy

I. Major Patrons

Ohio Joint Program in the Arts and Humanities
National Endowment for the Humanities
Marathon Oil Company Matching Grants
The University of Findlay:
   President Kenneth Zirkle
   Vice President John Scarpitti
   Dane Erford
   Rita Inman
   Mary Oakes
   John Hutson
The Courier Publishing and Commercial Printing, Findlay
Robert and Martha Bright
Joe La Forsch Jr.

Hotel de l'Annapurna, Kathmandu, Nepal.   Photo: Roger Sugden

Joy Lehmann
Elmer and Jean Graham
Westpac Banking Corporation
Bill and Jean Swales
Ivan and Dorothy Gorr
Richard and Beth Flowers
L. Don Manley
Don Badertscher
Jim and Patti Dimling
Mary and Sam Oakes
Walter Bovaird
Ed and Barbara Heminger
Jack Harrington

Dr. and Barbara Deerhake
Bill's Lock Service, Findlay
Margaret and Quenton Wood
Hotel de l'Annapurna, Kathmandu
Kathmandu Guest House, Kathmandu
Tibet House, New York
Office of Tibet, New York
Potala Travel and Tours, New Delhi
Overseas Adventure Travel, Kathmandu
Bob and Laura Calmus
Dow Chemical (Ziplock)
Dr. Pauline Hixson, Expedition Physician

The video *White Lotus* is made possible in part by the Ohio Joint Program in the Arts and Humanities. For further information about how this program can contribute to the cultural growth of your community, write to the Ohio Joint Programs, 65 Jefferson Ave., Columbus, Ohio 43215.

The video program is also made possible in part by the National Endowment for the Humanities.

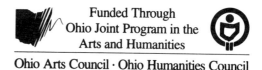

Funded Through
Ohio Joint Program in the
Arts and Humanities

Ohio Arts Council · Ohio Humanities Council

II. Very Special Thanks

His Holiness the Dalai Lama
Tenzin Geyche Tethong, Secretary to His Holiness
Sonam Topgyal, General Secretary, Information Office, Dharamsala
Tenpa C. Samkhar, Assistant to the General Secretary, Information Office
Representatives to His Holiness the Dalai Lama in New York, New Delhi, Kathmandu, Choglamsar, Ladakh, Bangalore, and Tokyo, especially Rinchen Dharlo, Tenzin Choedrak, Tempa Tsering, Tashi Wangdi, and Gyaltsen Lodoe
Tibet House, New Delhi
Ladakhi Gompa Society

Kathmandu Guest House, Kathmandu, Nepal.   Photo: Carole Elchert

Abbots of Sera Monastery: Geshe Lobsang Tsering, Geshe Drongrok, and Thek-
    chenling Lachi
Venerable K. C. Ayang Rinpoche, Kagyudpa Monastery
Geshe Ogyen Dorjee, Pangboche Monastery
Lama Nawang Tenzin Zangbu, Tyangboche Monastery
Tinley Lundrup and the monks of Tyangboche Monastery
Jamyang Tashi, Director, Majnu ka Tilla Camp, Delhi
Lama Wangchuck Gyaltsen and his family, Dharamsala
Karma Gyatsho and his family, Dharamsala
Sherab Choephell and Norzin Wangmo, Dehra Dun
Pasanng Tsering and Kalsang Choedon, Dharamsala
Karma Tenphal and Dolma, Leh, Ladakh
K. Yulgial and Lobsang Dhondup, Hunsur, India
Gyrmey Sonang and Karma, Potala Tours, Delhi
Lobsang Tenzin, Director, S.O.S. School, Ladakh
Tenzin Sangpo, Principal, S.O.S. School, Ladakh
Thubten Choeden, Ladakh
U.S.I.A., American Culture Center, Kathmandu
Ganesh Shankar lal Shrestha

Anna Souza
Robyn Brentano
Barbara Thompson
Dan Kelly
John and Belkiss Erickson
Bill Lammers

III. Patrons

Clayton Bash
Kani and David Meyers
Dave and Suzi Healey
Jerry Vossler
Joe Opperman
John and Patty Luther
Bev Fisher
Mr. and Mrs. Alan Struth
Bob and Linda Lotz
Bob and Margaret Ryan
Devere and Mary Line
Dr. and Phyliss Spragg
James K. and Virginia MacDonald
Dave and Marti Evans
Pat and Bill Stenzel
Lindy Demyan-Lehr and Steve Lehr
Margaret and Paul Palmer
Gwen and Howard Harris
Dr. Charles Dietz
Joe and Anita Marovich

James and Rebecca Kirk
Norm and Robin Richards
Marilyn Mallow
Bob and Connie Sprague
Jim Drake
Marge Weinrich
Jock and Margaret Maynard
Nan and Frank Guglielmi
George and PJ Milligan
Dr. and Mrs. Raymond Tille
Sally and Bill Robinson
Fostoria Industries
Al and Joanne Elchert
Blanchard Valley Medical Association
Ruth Dudley
Norman and Carol Roessing
Kurtis Leonard
Partricia Myers
Russell and Annette Elchert
Norris and Phyllis Roebuck
Simon and Martha Schalk
David and Dixie Stump
Orville Peterson
Loren and Charlotte Pace
Alexander and Mary Baluch
Joan Price
Lesley Clingerman
Eve Sugden
Louis and Irene Elchert
Nancy Sugden

Lama and Monk Recite Prayers at Spituk Monastery, Ladakh.
Photo: Philip Sugden